The God Who Plays

The God Who Plays

A Playful Approach to Theology and Spirituality

Brian Edgar

CASCADE *Books* • Eugene, Oregon

THE GOD WHO PLAYS
A Playful Approach to Theology and Spirituality

Cascade Books
An Imprint of Wipf and Stock Publishers
199 W. 8th Ave., Suite 3
Eugene, OR 97401

www.wipfandstock.com

PAPERBACK ISBN: 978-1-5326-0761-5
HARDCOVER ISBN: 978-1-5326-0763-9
EBOOK ISBN: 978-1-5326-0762-2

Cataloguing-in-Publication data:

Names: Edgar, Brian.

Title: The God who plays : a playful approach to theology and spirituality / Brian Edgar.

Description: Eugene, OR: Cascade Books, 2017 | Includes bibliographical references and index.

Identifiers: ISBN 978-1-5326-0761-5 (paperback) | ISBN 978-1-5326-0763-9 (hardcover) | ISBN 978-1-5326-0762-2 (ebook)

Subjects: LCSH: Play—Religious aspects—Christianity. | Theology—Relation to life. | Spirituality.

Classification: LCC BT709 E3 C58 2017 (print) | LCC E185.9.MBT7096 (ebook)

Manufactured in the U.S.A.   12/12/17

To Karly and Tara
in trust that they will play well

It is not only possible to say a great deal in praise of play; it is really possible to say the highest things in praise of it. It might reasonably be maintained that the true object of all human life is play. Earth is a task garden; heaven is a playground. To be at last in such secure innocence that one can juggle with the universe and the stars, to be so good that one can treat everything as a joke—that may be, perhaps, the real end and final holiday of human souls. When we are really holy we may regard the Universe as a lark.

—G. K. Chesterton

Contents

Preface

Over the course of writing this book it was always interesting—and often fun—to note the surprise on people's faces whenever I told them, usually in answer to a polite enquiry about what I was doing, that I was writing a book about play. One could see it on their faces as they wondered, and sometimes asked, "Is that a joke?"; "Why is someone who teaches theology writing about play?"; "Is this a book for children or adults?" These are all good questions: what, indeed, does theology or the Christian life have to with having fun or playing? One could spend quite some time in certain parts of the church without thinking that there was *any* connection at all.

The explanation then, as now, is that play is the essential and ultimate form of relationship with God. A playful attitude, I suggest, lies at the very heart of all spirituality and is critical for the whole of life. The idea that a playful attitude ought to be central to our relationship with God stands in sharp contrast with most common descriptions of the Christian life as a life of obedience to God and service of others, and thus a life characterized by duty, responsibility, commitment and other very serious attitudes, rather than by having fun and playing. This focus on steadfast commitment is, indeed, what happens when one focuses on the *present* Christian life, however, most depictions of the *future* kingdom of God describe that age very differently, in terms of joy, song, dance and even play. The question that then arises is whether the people of God—who are called to live out the future kingdom in the present age—ought not do more to demonstrate a life filled with joy, play and laughter, as well as with obedience and service. Indeed, in doing so one might well come to see more deeply the implications of the fact that the kind of personal relationship that God ultimately wants with people is one of play, joy and laughter.

The circumstances that brought the book about are described in chapter 1 but the fundamental reason for writing about play is simply the conviction that God wants to play. Our normal, everyday play is nothing other than a reflection of the relationship that God wants with us. A playful attitude lies at the heart of our relationship with God. Consequently, this book is not so much a theology of play as much as it is a playful theology. It is theology and the Christian life interpreted in the light of the concept of play and having a playful attitude. The individual chapters consider Christ, faith, grace, worship, theology, spirituality, love, redemption and kingdom in the light of an attitude of play.

In the preface to my book *God Is Friendship: A Theology of Spirituality, Community, and Society* (Seedbed 2013), I pointed out that my exploration of the theology of friendship was really the logical continuation of an earlier book on the theology of God as Trinity (*The Message of the Trinity*, InterVarsity 2004) and now I want to point out that this volume on the theology of play is really a further development of the same line of thought. One moves very naturally from a consideration of the implications of the communal life of God as *Trinity* to a reflection on the nature of *friendship* with God and others, and then to a discussion of *play* as a fundamental activity of those who are friends. Trinity, friendship and play are concepts that all stress the grace of God's desire for intimacy with people. (And the next logical step in this sequence of writing, it seems to me, is to write on the theology of laughter. I hope that will not be too far off.)

I am grateful to Asbury Theological Seminary, its president, Dr. Timothy Tennent, my colleagues on the faculty and the board of trustees for the semester sabbatical that enabled me to do much of the writing. It is a privilege to have time set apart for thought, study and writing. I am even more grateful to my wife, Barbara, who, as always, provides great love and support, and to my daughter Karly, who has been a tremendous help in the production of the manuscript.

All that remains is to trust that those who read this book will gain some insight into the nature of their relationship with God and the possibility of developing an attitude of joy and playfulness that will enhance their present life and be an integral part of the eternal life that is to come.

1

Christ: The God Who Plays

The true object of all human life is play.

—G. K. CHESTERTON

The central idea around which everything that follows revolves is the notion that *play is the essential and ultimate form of relationship with God.* A playful attitude, I suggest, lies at the very heart of all spirituality and is critical for the whole of life.

It is inevitable that some people will have difficulty in taking such a proposal seriously. But perhaps that is appropriate, not because play is trivial but because, as the great theorist of play Johan Huizinga argued, play is of a *higher* order than seriousness. Only a playful way of living, he suggested, does justice to the seriousness of life.[1]

However, the reality is that it is much more common for writers of books on Christian spirituality to discuss the spiritual significance of what appear to be much more serious concepts—such as servanthood, sacrifice, and commitment—rather than playfulness, games, and laughter. Consequently, when talking with people who are interested in what I am writing about it has often seemed necessary to justify the topic, as the concept of play is apparently so lightweight that it is difficult for many people to see the connection it has with the Christian life. This is partly because of the novelty of the idea and partly because there are a number of negative dimensions associated with play: it is often considered to be frivolous, sometimes inappropriate, and almost inevitably in our culture, always seen as secondary in value to work and service. Our cultural presuppositions about

1. Huizinga, *Homo Ludens*, 211–12.

play are ambivalent, to say the least, and the disconnect between play and church, or between play and spirituality, is comprehensive. The problem is compounded by the fact that there are a number of unhelpful assumptions about the metaphors that can appropriately be used to describe God. There is never a problem with the more transcendent terms such as Creator, King, Lord and Master but, for some people at least, it is more difficult to work with the more intimate descriptions of God as Lover, Friend, or even as Playmate. Consequently, any explanation about this book needs to involve the deconstruction of certain well-held assumptions.

Nonetheless, after the initial surprise the concept often becomes an interesting proposition because of the fun, the freedom, the pleasure and the adventure associated with play. Moreover, although the connection between play and spirituality has largely been lost by Western culture, there is nothing very original in developing an understanding of the playful dimension of life or spirituality, as this is an attitude to God and life that is found in both ancient philosophy and the biblical tradition. There is little claim for originality here except that there is a focus upon the needs of the present day, and in the contemporary world it is a rare thing to find *any* sustained theological reflection upon play or the spiritual importance of a playful attitude (or, perhaps to a lesser extent, its associated concepts such as humor, dance, creativity, relaxation, spontaneity and joy). A consideration of our relationship with God in terms of play involves some important implications for the way that we live with others. I want to suggest that Christians should take much more seriously the traditional understanding of the church, which interprets the future kingdom of God in terms of play, laughter, and dance, and to see the implications of this for three areas of life: (a) our present *relationship with God*, (b) the way we *interpret the world* today and (c) the most appropriate form of community life within *the church*.

Interpretations of Play

This is not the time for more than a brief recognition of the history of play but some context for the discussion will be helpful. Philosophical interpretations of life understood in terms of play go back as far as Plato (c. 427–347 B.C.), one of the principal founders of Western thought, who described humanity as being "God's plaything" and thus as having a responsibility to live playfully ("Life must be lived as play")[2] with others and God. The poet,

2. Plato, *Laws*, vii, 803 and 796.

playwright and philosopher Friedrich Schiller (1759–1805) famously argued that "man is only fully a human being when he plays"[3] and composer and philosopher Friedrich Nietzsche (1844–1900) utilized the term "play" to characterize a life that transcends the ethical categories of good and evil. Martin Heidegger (1889–1976) used the metaphor of play to explain the unique nature of human being and Hans-Georg Gadamer (1900–2002) used it to overcome the polarity of subject and object.

While the philosophers have their "players," theological interpretations of life and relationship with God in terms of play are relatively rare. It has been, at best, a minor theme, yet it is far from unknown. A considerable number of writers, theologians, mystics and pastors have noted the importance of play and its relationship with the sacred, but few have systematically explored it, despite frequently describing it as significant. Maximus the Confessor (c. 580–662) considered the fragility of life and observed that we "are like flowers which last but for a moment and then die and are transported into that other life—truly we deserve to be looked upon as a children's game played by God."[4] The great scholastic theologian Thomas Aquinas (1225–1274) argued that just as play is important for the body after it is tired from physical working, so too play is needed for the soul, which requires rest and relaxation from the even harder work of prayer. Thus play is to be commended.[5] He followed one of his heroes, Aristotle, in searching for a balance in life and so, while he saw certain forms of play as sinful (when senseless, hurtful or excessive), he also thought that a *lack* of play and laughter is sinful. He developed the theme by observing an even closer connection in that just as play gives pleasure the contemplation of wisdom gives the very greatest pleasure, and therefore is a form of play. His highest designation of God was, unusually but helpfully, as "Chief Friend"; he nonetheless did not explore the metaphor in terms of humanity doing what friends do—play—with God. That was, apparently, a step too far.

Others, however, have moved in that direction, including, much later, Friedrich Schiller, for whom the highest form of play is the contemplation of God.[6] For the Dominican mystic Meister Eckhardt (c. 1260–1327) the playing of Wisdom with the Lord at creation is an indication of an eternal, Trinitarian play of Father, Son and Holy Spirit. Theresa of Lisieux (1873–1897)

---

3. Schiller, *Aesthetic Education*, 107.
4. Rahner, *Play*, 25.
5. Aquinas, *Summa Theologica*, II–II, q. 168 , a. 2.
6. Schiller, *Aesthetic Education*, 107.

expressed a modest desire to participate in the play of God by being a toy, a little ball for the infant Christ.[7] Romano Guardini (1885–1968) defended both the "uselessness" and the profundity of play and worship in his study of liturgy as play[8] and Hugo Rahner (1900–1968), in a rare and detailed exposition, explored the Christian life entirely in terms of a playfulness that arises from the freedom of a God who plays. "Mere seriousness," he argued, does not get down to the roots of things. There is a sacred secret in play which is the hope for another form of life. All play arises from the human longing for the vision of the divine.[9]

The reality, however, is that the church's tradition has more commonly taken a negative view of play. Among the fathers, for example, Ambrose of Milan (c. 340–397) frequently quoted the Lord Jesus as saying, "woe to you who laugh, for you shall weep" (Luke 6:25) and told his people that all games should be avoided. The great preacher and archbishop of Constantinople John Chrysostom (c. 347–407) wrote,

> This world is not a theatre, in which we can laugh; and we are not assembled together in order to burst into peals of laughter, but to weep for our sins. But some of you still want to say: "I would prefer God to give me the chance to go on laughing and joking." Is there anything more childish than thinking this way? It is not God who gives us the chance to play, but the devil.[10]

In short, the Christian focus has tended to fall upon service and work rather than play, and upon activity in general rather than rest. As the Puritan Richard Baxter said, "it is for action that God maintaineth us and our activities," and as the well-known saying puts it, "the devil finds work for idle hands." But playfulness, delight and joy ought to characterize the nature of the Christian and his or her relationship with God. While there is every reason to affirm and maintain concepts such as ministry, service, obedience, sacrifice, duty, work and responsibility, it is unhelpful, in our perceptions of our lives and relationships, to substitute them for those dimensions of life and relationship that are central to the future life of the eschaton. In seeking to describe the future life the Christian tradition consistently turns to the metaphors of play, music and dance. Zechariah 8:3–5 describes the heavenly city as a place filled with children playing, a theme that is, of

7. Knox, *Autobiography of a Saint*, 171.

8. Guardini, *Spirit of the Liturgy*, 37–45.

9. Rahner, *Man at Play*, 65.

10. Chrysostom, *Homilies*, 6, 70D.

course, picked up by the Lord Jesus, who said that the kingdom belongs "to such as these" (Matt 19:14). It is important to take seriously the significance of this eschatological play for the believer's present relationship with God. Wolfhart Pannenberg commented that it was only relatively recently, in the twentieth century, that "theology has come to see again the significance of the theme of eschatology for all Christian doctrine."[11]

There was a time when thinking eschatologically meant thinking about the events at the end of human history—the return of Christ, judgment, the consummation of all things, heaven and hell—as a distinct category events that followed on from consideration of other doctrines such as the doctrine of God, Christology, the atonement, the life of church and so forth. But eschatological thinking that follows a biblical mode of thought really means allowing the final events, the end purpose of all things, to influence one's understanding of all preceding doctrines and events, including the form of the present life of the believer. What then does it mean for today that the ultimate relationship that believers have with God is expressed in terms of play, song and dance?

The Forgotten Virtue

An exploration of life with God understood in terms of playfulness means that although this is a book about play it is not about games or playing so much as about *an attitude of life*, a way of living in relationship with God and others. Now, it has to be admitted immediately that "play" and "playfulness" are likely to be misunderstood, but it is difficult to find alternatives. The Greeks had a special word for understanding this—*eutrapelia*—which has the distinct advantage of sounding so much more serious for a concept that is described as central to the spiritual life of the believer. *Eutrapelia*, as the philosophers understood it, describes the balanced attitude that involves an *appropriate* level of playfulness (neither constant jocularity nor unmitigated seriousness) and it was considered to be among the essential virtues. More will be said later about the philosophical concept of *eutrapelia* and of the need to relate it to biblical material, nonetheless it does express something about an appropriate *lightness of being*, which, in Christian terms, can refer to the balance between work and play, between seriousness and fun, and between the responsibilities of ministry and the joy of worship.

11. Pannenberg, *Systematic Theology*, 3:532.

The concept of *eutrapelia,* incidentally, provides an answer to the important theological question, "Why is it that angels can fly?" And the answer is, "Because they take themselves lightly." Which is good advice for us all. And it is a truth about life that could have been made by reference to a biblical text as easily as by reference to a joke, but anyone who insists on the former is in danger of missing an essential point about the theology of play! Any serious theological exploration of the spiritual significance of play needs to avoid the charge of being dull. Serious it may be, but not dull. In his typically ironic way G. K. Chesterton "apologized" for the state of the essays collected from various newspapers in his *All Things Considered* because of the time pressure that had been involved in producing comments on very topical issues. "Their chief vice," he observed, "is that so many of them are serious; because I had no time to make them flippant. It is so easy to be solemn; it is so hard to be frivolous."[12]

A lot of theological writing reads not only as very serious but also as quite dull, except perhaps to those who, for whatever reason, are completely devoted to theological writing and know how to deal with just about anything. There are, after all, geeks in every area of life! *Mea culpa.* But how does one write theology playfully? With chapters presented randomly and with cryptic clues as to the right sequence? With jokes? Or with a board game attached? One should certainly follow the example of the angels and not take oneself too seriously. But the best approach, as with any form of play, is to be fully engaged with a playmate, a partner, someone to play with, because it is of the essence of play that one engages with another. In this book I trust that there will be some engagement with the reader, but there is also a playful engagement with God, and the following account of the way in which this book came to be written illustrates the point.

I enjoy looking around bookshops, and that includes those ones that are often found in temporary accommodation—in shops or factories that are in between leases to permanent businesses—where they have stacks of remaindered books all going for just a few dollars. It provides one with the opportunity to pick up large numbers of substantial books on various topics of possible interest very cheaply when one might otherwise hesitate to pay full price. Once, as I was looking around I saw a substantial book by Pat Kane with the title *The Play Ethic.* I took an interest in this even before I picked it up because it was immediately apparent that this was not a book about the ethics of play but was, much more broadly, an exploration of a

12. Chesterton, *All Things Considered,* 1.

play ethic that, I thought, would be a very useful counter to the very much more common *work ethic* that influences so much of our society. So I purchased the book and during the next week proceeded to read it and make some theological applications to what was a purely secular analysis of play. This, it should be noted, was the first time in my life that I had ever considered a theology of play. A week later I was halfway through the book when I received a letter from a former colleague, the biblical scholar Joel Green, who was writing as the general editor of what was to become the *Dictionary of Scripture and Ethics*,[13] and he asked whether I would be willing to write an article on "play" for the dictionary! I have no idea why he would think to ask me to write on that topic. There was no way that he could have known of my very recent theological reflections on play, let alone of any previous writing on the subject because there simply weren't any. And the decision to ask me to write that article must have been made just before I saw Kane's book. Theologically, what does this mean? Of course, one could put it down to coincidence, but when I received the letter it seemed to me that I had no choice but to accept: it had been made very clear to me by a coincidence of the Spirit that I was to write that article. Now some might well ask whether it is theologically appropriate to think that God would arrange such a trivial matter in this kind of way, and it is, after all, possible to read too much into circumstances, especially of the relatively trivial kind. But then again, who knows exactly what is to be considered trivial (it has, after all, led to considerable changes for me), moreover it seems very appropriate to me to believe that God should engage me in this way in regard to the topic of play. When I put it to other colleagues they laughed and said, "God is playing with you!" It certainly does make the point that there is a real sense in which God plays with us. And the emphasis here falls on the "with" because in playing with us God is not "toying" with anyone, but engaging with us in free, creative, enjoyable play. As one does with one's friends.

All Work and No Play . . .

The importance of play is suggested in the proverb, "All work and no play makes Jack a dull boy," and it is true that a life of work without play is psychologically disastrous. Of course, the play dimension can, for some people at least, be found within their work. For others, however, either their internal attitude to work or the nature of the work itself makes it necessary for play

13. Edgar, *Play*, 595–96.

to be a separate activity. But whether play is found in the work itself or in a separate activity, a complete absence of play will result in far more than dullness: it will almost inevitably develop into full-blown depression. A certain playfulness in life is needed by all and it would be possible to think and write extensively on this issue alone, but from a more specifically spiritual point of view I want to ask, what is a Christian life of work, service, sacrifice and worship like without play? The reality is that in a spiritual context the absence of play has even more negative results. A life of Christian ministry, service, sacrifice and worship that does not embody, as part of it, the joy and delight of a playful relationship with God will become a duty-bound and moralistic life that will have difficulty in developing a close, intimate relationship with the one who is our chief and best Friend. This is because a playful attitude lies at the heart of all close relationships. The absence of this kind of relationship has meant burnout for far too many Christians. Just as in everyday life work without play makes one dull, in the Christian life service without a playful relationship with God leads to spiritual dullness.

It is not uncommon for Christians to take Paul's words "continue to work out your salvation with fear and trembling" (Phil 2:12) out of context and to understand it as implying a very unplayful state of nervous anxiety. But Philippians is "the epistle of joy" and Paul is clear that as his readers continue to press on towards holiness they "should be glad and rejoice with me" (v. 18). The "fear and trembling" indicates a state of complete dependency upon God, "for it is God who works in you." The gospel is, fundamentally, nothing other than "good news" and a message "of great joy" (Luke 2:10). A playful dimension to life is important for everyone and it may be expressed in many ways (from playing instruments to puzzling over cryptic cross-words to going to the theatre) but it is not (only) this kind of play that is needed in one's spiritual life. These relieve psychological dullness and enhance one's living of everyday life, but the spiritual life needs a more specifically spiritual play that is a way of relating to God, others and the world with a joy and delight that goes beyond the pleasures of bingo, ball games, or backgammon.

So much good and helpful material has been written about the way in which a mature relationship with God may develop that one is almost apologetic for daring to add to it, especially when the emphasis falls upon concepts, such as friendship and play, that appear to be so simple. Suggesting that the way to develop spiritually is to have fun with *God* seems to run counter to much that one finds implied elsewhere. But the notion that we would do well to perceive a mature relationship with Christ in terms of friendship and play is important. There is no time when we are as full of life as when we play! Play, or one might say a "playful attitude," is at the heart of religious experience.

Play in the spiritual realm has the same qualities that play has at any time: it does not deal with what *is*, but rather with what *could be*. It always involves another, transcendent world or sphere of meaning. Play transcends immediate reality and takes one into another world. Play is the spontaneous expression of a free spirit, of something done purely and only because one wants to do it. There is no compulsion, for no one can be forced to play. And there are no ulterior motives in play—it is done only for its own sake. The one playing simply takes pleasure and delight in the playing. A playful spiritual life is one that emphasizes joy, delight, freedom, grace and love. Really, play is too good to be left to children!

Let us reject any thought that play is childish in the sense that it is something out of which one eventually grows. Understanding that involves a great freedom. I always appreciated a sign that I once saw hanging in a friend's house: "When I grow up I want to be a kid!" That is, of course, a very biblical attitude. The kingdom of heaven "belongs to such as these" for very good reason (Matt 19:14)! Let's take being childish seriously and learn from them, rather than expect them to learn from adults. Unfortunately, this has sometimes not been understood. John Wesley is quoted as saying about Methodist schools,

> we prohibit play in the strongest terms . . . The students shall rise at 5 o'clock in the morning, summer and winter . . . The student shall be indulged with nothing which the world calls play. But this rule be observed with strictest nicety; for those who play when they are young will play when they are old.[14]

How much better if the adults learned from the children! The spiritual life should be an adventure of faith involving all the characteristics of adventurous play: suspense and surprise, drama and danger, risk and reward, fun and freedom. It may not seem that way to someone who looks on from the outside, but it is the inner dynamics that are the essence of it all. G. K. Chesterton had it right when he said,

> It is not only possible to say a great deal in praise of play; it is really possible to say the highest things in praise of it. It might reasonably

14. Wesley, "Short Account of the School in Kingswood," 98.

be maintained that the true object of all human life is play. Earth is a task garden; heaven is a playground. To be at last in such secure innocence that one can juggle with the universe and the stars, to be so good that one can treat everything as a joke—that may be, perhaps, the real end and final holiday of human souls. When we are really holy we may regard the universe as a lark.[15]

Prayer as a Form of Play

Reading the detailed and intense philosophical arguments in Thomas Aquinas's *Summa Theologica* can easily lead one to assume that this influential medieval theologian was a devoted but somewhat dour disciple. Yet he recognized the spiritual benefits of a playful attitude both in life and in relationship with God. Indeed, rather than merely defending the concept he threw out a challenge to common thinking and asked whether it was not sinful *not* to play. In his inevitably thorough manner he also asked whether it was possible for there to be an excess of play (which could lead to its own form of sinfulness), but he was certainly concerned with making the point that there was sin in not playing.[16] One might call this the sin of seriousness, a counterpart to the sin of an excess of levity.

In considering the merits and pitfalls of play Aquinas was not only showing that play is an activity that has spiritual implications in the ordinary activities of life; he was, even more importantly, also deliberately laying the groundwork for a positive view of play as intrinsic to a life of contemplative prayer. He demonstrated that there can be an excess of play in various ways, as when it is discourteous, insolent, scandalous or obscene, and that there is such a thing as fun at the wrong time or place. He followed Augustine in arguing that play can be wasteful, as when one spends money on entertainment that could be given to those in hunger. But despite these qualifications about inappropriate play, and despite the influence of Augustine's general reservations about play, and even despite his affirmation of the importance of austerity, Aquinas also reckoned, with Aristotle, that play is a virtue and that a lack of fun in life is a vice. It is wrong, Aquinas argued, to fail to offer pleasure to others, to hinder their enjoyment of life and to be "without mirth" or "lacking in playful speech." He commended (with temperance) affability, friendliness, wittiness and

15. Chesterton, *All Things Considered*, 40.
16. Aquinas, *Summa Theologica*, II–II, q. 168, a. 2.

play. So much did Aquinas value playfulness that he argued the one who does *not* play risks falling into sin.

Yet this affirmation of play as a part of life was not the main point that Aquinas was seeking to make. Having established the value and virtue of play and laughter as a common activity of daily life, he then went further and discerned in play something more essential and more spiritual. The second stage in Aquinas's observation about play is that it is parallel in nature to contemplative prayer. He argued that there are two comparisons to be made between play and prayer that go to the very essence of play. Both play and "the contemplation of wisdom" are undertaken purely for their own sake, with no other motive or function in mind, and both play and the contemplation of wisdom are done solely for pleasure. Consequently, for Aquinas, there is no surprise that Proverbs 8 describes the joy of the Eternal Wisdom present with God at the creation of the universe as a form of play. In this Aquinas was following the tradition that includes the teaching of Maximus the Confessor, who worked out an entire mystical theology of a playing God for whom both creation and incarnation are playful expressions of God's love. God enables people who have learned to play in ordinary ways to understand and recognize him in divine playfulness. Proverbs 8 provides only a hint of the eternal playfulness that has taken place since before the beginning of time and which will be revealed at the end of time.[17]

The third stage of Aquinas's argument is that play is not only parallel in nature to prayer but is a correlate of contemplative prayer. That is, their characteristics cannot only be compared, they are connected. As a point of comparison, modern thought typically correlates play with work rather than with prayer. Work and play are seen as different yet connected activities. They are different in that play is what one does for pleasure while work is essentially productive in nature. They can, of course, overlap for those who are able to treat work as play but they are always correlated in that play is seen as an essential break from work and an important way of refreshing oneself for further work. This connection between work and play is one to which we will return later. At this point is sufficient to note that Aquinas also made this connection between work and play but also that what was more significant to him is the way that play has a connection with prayer— a point that contemporary Christians perhaps ought to note with care. "Just as man needs bodily rest . . . so too is it with his soul if the soul be occupied with the work of contemplation . . . weariness of the soul must needs be

17. Louth, *Maximus*, 163–68.

11

remedied by resting the soul: and the soul's rest is pleasure."[18] The pleasure that refreshes the soul is playful and humorous and this enables one to return to contemplative prayer—rather than merely to work.

Although Aquinas had taken some important steps in understanding the spiritual value of play by relating it to prayer, he did not go nearly as deeply into the matter as he could have, despite the fact that he prepared the way for an even more intimate relationship between play and prayer. Let me add another dimension to this connection between play and prayer. Firstly, learning to play enables one to pray because it creates the capacity for exploring other worlds beyond the one immediately present to us. It is well understood that in terms of human development play is critical, whether one considers it socially (Erikson), cognitively (Piaget), intrapsychically (Freud) or morally (Kohlberg). But play is also central in spiritual development. Through play children, adolescents and adults not only learn about themselves, their environment and others, they also gain a capacity that facilitates learning about God—that is, they develop their own inner, subjective life that interacts with others (both pretend and real) and opens up the possibility of an inner, interactive, spiritual life. Healthy play depends on the capacity to be alone. Playing helps develop this and provides a way for a person to learn to relate and reflect subjectively. An inability to be alone creates a pathological situation where the individual is entirely subject to the need to continually respond to external stimuli or to be frustrated when unable to find suitable external activity. This builds reactivity rather than creativity and playfulness. Leading play theorist Brian Sutton-Smith argues that "what may be most important in all of this is the benefit play affords each child, who gains confidence in a variety of these play pretense forms and thereby develops an inner, subjective life, a life that becomes the child's own relatively private possession."[19]

All play, but especially pretend forms of play, develops the ability to engage with others (real persons as well as imaginary) and to sustain this interaction through the whole process of a game. It also develops the ability to recognize and understand different rules of play and relationships and, especially, to gain and give pleasure in relating with another. Having an imaginary friend, for example, requires a certain sense of self and the ability to distinguish oneself from an interacting other because to play in this way it is necessary to be able to play both roles and keep them separate.

18. Aquinas, *Summa Theologica*, II-II, q. 168, a. 2.

19. Sutton-Smith, "Play Theory," 118.

Play develops the ability to perceive situations and feelings from someone else's point of view. In short, play creates a subjective life and opens up the possibility of an inner, spiritual life. Without the ability to play one cannot develop the ability to pray.

This learning to play and pray is not only related to childhood. In having a playful attitude throughout life we are continually learning about new possibilities. Playing is not only good for developing mental and emotional health but spiritual health as well. The endpoint of this connection between play and prayer is not merely that they share similar characteristics or even that play is a normal developmental preparation for prayer, but rather that *prayer is a form of play*. It involves the freedom, the lack of obligation, the dynamic interaction and the joy and pleasure of play. In this world there is always an end to a game but prayer is a preparation for the eternal game which has no end. And it is something that, as we shall see, is best learned from children.

Playing with the Idea of Play

Playing through Thinking and Prayer

At the end of each chapter there will be some ideas about exploring play in your life. There is, after all, an intellectual interest in the theology of play but without some engagement in actual practice it will be deficient.

Start by asking about your own attitude towards play. Do you enjoy playing? What kind of games do you particularly like? Do you see yourself having a playful attitude towards others and God? How would you describe the nature of your relationship with God? Has play been a part of your experience with God? Can you see examples of God playing with you?

Aquinas saw a relationship between prayer and play. What would it mean you would do if you took a play attitude into your prayer for, say, the next week?

2

Faith: It's Child's Play!

At that time Jesus said, "I praise you, Father, Lord of heaven and earth, because you have hidden these things from the wise and learned, and revealed them to little children."

MATTHEW 11:25

Let the little children come to me, and do not hinder them, for the kingdom of God belongs to such as these. Truly I tell you, anyone who will not receive the kingdom of God like a little child will never enter it."

LUKE 18:16

Several thousand years ago in the Middle East there was a king who, unusually for the age, deliberately rejected the arbitrary use of earthly power and authority and instead handed it over to others. He developed a reputation and was widely known as a wise man and a teacher, although his teaching subverted many common views about life. He reflected publicly on the nature of the world, the Word (Logos) and eternal life. He enjoyed the company of children and he declared that "the kingdom belongs to a child."

And, despite the similarities, this particular teacher of wisdom was *not* Jesus of Nazareth but Heraclitus of Ephesus. [1]

---

1. Hippolytus of Rome, *Refutation of All Heresies*, book 9, ch. 4.

Heraclitus, a Greek philosopher and king, lived more than five hundred years before Jesus. He was known as "the Weeping Philosopher" because of his pessimistic view of life and it appears that he abdicated his throne in favor of his brother. He is most famous for saying, "No man ever steps in the same river twice"[2] in order to stress the ever-changing nature of the whole of life. His reference to the kingdom belonging to a child is recorded in the writings of various church fathers, including Hippolytus of Rome (c. 170–235), who was keen to demonstrate that Heraclitus' teaching about the Logos and the kingdom confirmed Christian thought. This was stretching the similarities a bit much but, nonetheless, Heraclitus certainly used imagery about children and the kingdom that was similar to what Jesus said, quite independently, centuries later, such that "anyone who will not receive the kingdom of God like a little child will never enter it . . . for of such is the kingdom of God."

According to Jesus one cannot understand life in the kingdom of God without understanding the way that children enter into it and, as we shall see, this is connected with an affirmation of the way that children live and play. Adults have much to learn from children about the way that life in the kingdom is to be lived. The playful life of children is an example for everyone. But, unfortunately, there has been significant resistance to this childish and playful approach to the kingdom. People have persistently resisted the subversive wisdom of Jesus, which not only insists that "the first shall be last" and that "the greatest among you will be the least" but also that adults should learn from children (rather than the more customary state of children learning from adults) and that a spirituality of play is to be preferred to one of self-denial.

This resistance to childishness and playfulness started at the time Jesus began teaching and healing. Luke's gospel (7:18–33) describes the way that the news about Jesus spread throughout Judea and the surrounding country. John the Baptist heard about it and sent two of his disciples to ask Jesus, "Are you the one who is to come, or should we expect someone else?" Jesus' response to this uncertainty on the part of John and the others about the significance of his ministry was to say, "I praise you, Father, Lord of heaven and earth, because you have hidden these things from the wise and learned, and revealed them to little children." The deeds that Jesus did spoke for themselves ("The blind receive sight, the lame walk, those who have leprosy are cleansed, the deaf hear, the dead are raised, and the good

2. Plato, *Cratylus*, 402a.

news is proclaimed to the poor") and it should have been obvious that God was involved in them, but there were doubts and Jesus contrasted the attitude of the allegedly wise and learned people unfavorably with the much more receptive attitude of children.

The uncertainty of John the Baptist was, however, nothing compared with the outright resistance of the Pharisees and the experts in the law. They rejected God's purposes and saw nothing good in either John or Jesus. Jesus went on to describe both himself and John as children sitting in the marketplace who had called on other children to join them in their games, but they were both rejected: "We played the flute for you, and you did not dance; we sang a dirge and you did not cry." That is to say, "the people of this generation" rejected both the austere John and the celebratory Jesus. John the Baptist had come "neither eating bread nor drinking wine" and the Pharisees and experts in the law said he was possessed by a demon. Jesus had come "eating and drinking" and they said he was a glutton and a drunkard. They rejected both and would not play with either of them.

Ascetic and Aesthetic Spiritualities

John and Jesus played different tunes but they both brought to people the possibility of meeting with God. Their different approaches were not contradictory. As Jesus said, "wisdom is proved right by all her children" (Luke 7:35). John exemplified an ascetic or disciplined approach to finding the way to God in fasting and austerity, denial and sacrifice, and in withdrawal and solitude. John may be seen as representative of an approach to the spiritual life that has always been profoundly influential. It involves disengagement from the world in order to engage fully with God, and in the early church it was seen as the most effective way of being assured of salvation. An ascetic life was the mark of every true Christian. But Jesus himself, in contrast to John, exemplified an aesthetic or playful approach to life and ministry. He came eating and drinking and expressing a full appreciation for life and all that it contains. This is an approach to the spiritual life that stresses the beauty and goodness of God's creation and complete engagement with the world. It involves an appreciation of art, an attitude of playfulness and an outlook permeated with deep joy.

Although their different approaches were not contradictory, the fact that John and Jesus played such different tunes means that it is perhaps no surprise that some of John's disciples thought that Jesus was a competitor and complained, "Rabbi, that man who was with you on the other side of the Jordan—the one you testified about—look, he is baptizing, and everyone is going to him." But John understood more than they did and pointed out that he, John, was not the Messiah, but only one who had been sent ahead of him. He was more like the friend of the bridegroom who prepares things and then waits for the groom's arrival. His role was to be disciplined in preparation; the real joy was to occur when the groom himself arrived to take his bride (John 3:29–30). John the disciplined ascetic was to prepare the way for the joy of the Messiah's coming.

It is possible to characterize the two spiritualities demonstrated by John and Jesus by saying that the ascetic approach stresses the work of atonement and the defeat of sin (appropriate for John as he was preparing for the sacrificial offering of the one he described as "the Lamb of God") while the aesthetic approach stresses the goodness of creation and the joy of salvation (in which Jesus was anticipating the joyful life of the kingdom that was to come). The ascetic approach remains important as Christians continue to live in this world and need to constantly be reminded of the need to reject everything that detracts from union with God, but the aesthetic approach is a reflection of the final state that will be achieved in the kingdom of God. It is particularly here that we need to learn about play from children. The adults who opposed Jesus simply would not play and so they could not experience the joy of salvation. And the point here is not about playing a particular game; it has much more to do with an attitude to God and to the life God gives.

Play is pleasure and in the kingdom of God a theology of enjoyment and pleasure is important. In practice, however, Christians are more used to being encouraged to lives of service and sacrifice and to avoid self-indulgence and pleasure. This is because of the need to avoid believing one can find life's ultimate pleasure in anything other than God. It is undoubtedly the case that the only ultimate pleasure lies in the enjoyment of God, but the question then is whether one is helped in this by denying other pleasures—the route of the ascetic—or by experiencing them—the route of the aesthete. In his spiritual autobiography Augustine famously distinguished between "lower goods" and "higher goods" and argued that each ought to be loved according to its nature.[3] A lower good should not be loved as though it was higher good. The lower goods are only pleasurable

---

3. Augustine of Hippo, *Confessions*, book 2.

because God made them that way and they are only rightly enjoyed if they are enjoyed in God, rather than independently of God.

But what does it mean to enjoy them "in God"? What does this look like in real life? Jesus' answer to this is to direct our attention to children.

> People were bringing little children to Jesus for him to place his hands on them, but the disciples rebuked them. When Jesus saw this, he was indignant. He said to them, "Let the little children come to me, and do not hinder them, for the kingdom of God belongs to such as these. Truly I tell you, anyone who will not receive the kingdom of God like a little child will never enter it." And he took the children in his arms, placed his hands on them and blessed them. (Mark 10:13–16)

Adults can grow in the understanding of their spiritual relationship with God by focusing more on the faith of children, but it is easy for adult interpreters of Jesus to unconsciously consider adult concerns ahead of those of children. In doing so people are sometimes too literal in their interpretation of Jesus' words about children. In the sixteenth century there were Anabaptists who, in response to the words of Jesus about receiving the kingdom like a child, ran around playing with hoops and toys and making noises like babies. It is good to take the words of Jesus very seriously, but not so literally! Jesus' words are not instructions about adults mimicking children in this way. At other times, in avoiding this kind of literalism interpreters have been too metaphorical and have argued that the children are merely illustrations of the main point about the way that the kingdom belongs to those adults who are like children. Consequently, either the status of children is considered to not be the point or, even worse, children are assumed to not actually be in the kingdom at all, at least not until they achieve an age when they can put themselves into the kingdom by having faith in Jesus (which, ironically, happens when one is an adult who has faith like a child!). Both these approaches are focused on adult concerns and should be resisted.

Childish Faith

Adult-focused thinking, in which neither children nor play are part of the kingdom, is by no means universal, but it has been a common part of Christian tradition that extends back to the earliest days. The early Greek fathers of the church, such as Gregory of Nyssa (c. A.D. 330–395) and Gregory of Nazianzus (A.D. 329–389), for example, expressed a certain agnosticism about the spiritual state of children who died, but they certainly did not see children as being at the heart of the kingdom of God. Children were not considered liable to punishment as they had not sinned personally but nor were they considered to have achieved the same state of eternal life in the kingdom of God as "those who have been purified in this life by all the virtues."[4] Their eternal status was considered something of a mystery.

In the early church of the West the spiritual status of children became tied up with the Pelagian debate concerning free will and grace. Around the end of the fourth century Pelagius argued that infants who died without baptism were not personally guilty of sin and so could enter into "eternal life" but not into the "kingdom of God." Augustine argued in response that unbaptized children are consigned to hell. The fact that they were, in his day, being baptized as part of the normal course of events was proof to him that they were sinful and needed to be removed from the threat of hell and brought into the kingdom of God. Although they may not have personally sinned they had sinned "in Adam" (1 Cor 15:22) and so, if God condemns children it is because they are sinners, even though their punishment may be "the lightest punishment of all."[5]

Augustine's authority was so great that many of the other fathers (including Jerome and Gregory the Great and the Western church generally) followed his teaching although there was a later tendency to stress the mildness of their punishment or even, according to both Thomas Aquinas (c. 1225–1274) and Duns Scotus (c. 1265–1308), to argue that they could ultimately enjoy a certain happiness and a union with God in a "natural," though not a "supernatural," way.[6] It has been pretty hard, however, for the theology of children to recover from treatment such as this and consequently children have often, though by no means always, been seen as spiritually lost rather than as the first in the kingdom. But there are two reasons for understanding what Jesus says as meaning that all children belong to the kingdom of God. Firstly, the words of Jesus are clear. What he says in Luke 18:16 about the kingdom belonging "to such as these" (*toiouton*) is expressed in the same way that the mob respond to Paul's teaching in Acts 22:22 by crying out "away with such a one" (*toioutōv*). It would be absurd to assume that they wanted to get rid of other people who preached in this way but not Paul. Obviously, Paul was the first person they wanted

4. International Theological Commission, *Hope of Salvation*, para. 12.

5. Ibid., para. 15.

6. Ibid., para. 16.

removed, and then if there were others they wanted them removed as well. Similarly, it is a distorted adult interpretation that argues that the kingdom belongs to those who are like children, but not firstly to actual children themselves. Secondly, the notion that children are an example of the way that adults can enter God's kingdom can, logically, only be valid because the kingdom actually belongs to children in the first place. They cannot be illustrations of entering the kingdom if they do not enter it.

Much more moderate forms of resistance to learning from children show in what one usually reads in systematic theology textbooks about entering the kingdom of God. They typically discuss "the order of salvation" in terms of repentance, regeneration, faith, conversion, baptism in the Spirit, justification, union, sanctification and so forth. Here the usual standard is the experience of an adult coming to faith, whereas for Jesus the best example was a child. These more formal theological descriptions of the necessity for repentance, faith, justification, sanctification and union will then, at a later point in the text, frequently have to address the issues relating to the place of children in the kingdom and whether they fit the template that has been established earlier in the discussion of the order of salvation. The answer may well be that children, by the grace of God and according to the words of Jesus about children and the kingdom of God, are indeed recipients of salvation even though they do not consciously follow the established pattern, but they are still the ones who have to fit into an adult schema.

Faith is essential in order for anyone to enter the kingdom of God. The apostle Paul reminded believers of this when he said, "it is by grace you have been saved, through faith," and the writer of the epistle to the Hebrews observed that "without faith it is impossible to please God" (Eph 2:8; Heb 11:6), and it is precisely in this that adults are told to become like children: "unless you change and become like little children, you will never enter the kingdom of heaven" (Matt 18:3). There are not, of course, two ways into the kingdom, one for adults and one for children; there is only one and it is usually well described theologically in the textbooks in terms of "by grace through faith" and involving repentance, regeneration, justification and the rest, but the best example of this, according to the Lord Jesus, is typically neglected.

Resistance to learning from children comes quite naturally for two reasons. Firstly, it seems to make sense to most adults to learn from the greatest, the best, the wisest people that they know, and for Christians this means finding teachers and mentors who are most mature in faith and those who are spiritually strong, rather than looking towards children. Secondly, it is widely assumed that children are to be students, rather than teachers, of adults. It is assumed that they need to be taught and helped by those that have already learned something of life and faith. Overall, it is hard for adults to learn from children but, ironically, this resistance is evidence of the very need for it because there are two things adults need to learn from children, and the first is the humility that comes with being vulnerable and completely dependent upon someone else. The second is the total commitment to life that children express in every facet of their being. These are the personal building blocks that go towards establishing the faith by which every person must enter the kingdom of God.

The first of these building blocks—the humility that comes with vulnerability and dependence upon someone else—is integral to the life of a small child. Children are completely vulnerable in that they rely totally and absolutely on others—mothers, fathers, family, society—for everything. They receive the kingdom in the same way that they receive life itself: as a gift that they have not sought. Children are the finest examples of entering the kingdom of God because their faith is so unconscious, so natural, so much a part of their lives that, unlike adults, they are not encouraged to "have" it because they cannot possibly be without it! And, unlike adults, they are not warned about losing it because it is so intrinsic to their life and being. When Jesus used children as an example of those in the kingdom he was not referring to some particular, special group of children, but to all. The faithfulness that children exhibit is not a quality that some have and others don't; it is simply inherent in who they are. Children should not be idealized as though they were chosen because they are good in some sense—they are not always good or completely perfect or righteous—but they do come with completely empty hands and without any of the rationalizations, justifications, explanations or excuses that are found in adults. As such, children are living illustrations of justification by grace and the best examples of the way into the kingdom of God.

In order for adults to become like children they have to demonstrate the same reliance upon God. This is expressed in biblical teaching in various ways. Paul declared to the Philippians that it was imperative for him to divest himself not only of the worst aspects of his life, but of any reliance on the very best as well. Whatever gains he had in regard to his faultless obedience to the law he later regarded as a loss, mere garbage.

He came "not having a righteousness of my own that comes from the law, but that which is through faith in Christ" (Phil 3:9). The parables of Jesus also reinforce the message that it is precisely the least deserving, and those who have achieved the least, who are to be the recipients of grace: in prayer it is the repentant tax collector and not the pious Pharisee that is justified. The guests at the great banquet are the poor and the crippled and the lame rather than the wealthy. And the worker who only worked for one hour receives a full day's pay. According to the standards of the world this teaching does not appropriately reward effort and labor and it frequently appears to be unjust, but Jesus calls us to leave behind the usual expectations of the adult world. Children quite naturally accept the grace of God, but for adults the only way forward is to start all over, to be born again and to become a child of God.

So, if the first step in learning from children involves the negation of self-achievement and an acceptance of complete vulnerability, then the second step is simply the corollary to this; it is the positive and enthusiastic embrace of life with God. This is critical because vulnerability is by no means the only important characteristic of childhood. Indeed, this is not the way children perceive their life. It may be their objective state, but it is not always their subjective awareness. Whatever they do, children live and experience life fully in the present, without reserve. They cannot but be committed to life. Whether laughing or crying, playing or sleeping, eating or dirtying their nappy, the experience of life is all-consuming for them.

In contrast, the adult tendency is to examine life, to reflect on it and compare, assess and judge it. In many respects this is a very good thing; as Plato famously observed, the unexamined life is not worth living. But at the same time it brings in all the typically adult rationalizations, reservations, justifications and excuses that end up detracting from the experience of life itself. Children, on the other hand, exhibit none of these, and the contrast between the life of a child and that of an adult perhaps shows up most clearly in one of the main characteristics of children: that of play.

Play is the most perfect expression of the life of the one completely reliant upon the grace of God. In playing there is no thought of the production of any "thing" for the common good, no sense of the need to "do something" that will justify one's existence, and play is not an expression of an innate sense of responsibility for caring for oneself or the life of others. Yet God calls us to this childish way of life, a way of living that is characterized by play, and although it is childish it is by no means trivial. Those Anabaptists at least understood that child's play was an important affirmation of life, even though they took it too literally. Perhaps they are at least closer to the truth than those who will not accept the notion of a playful God.

The German philosopher Friedrich Nietzsche (1844–1900), who is usually known as an atheist, perhaps demonstrated a more subtle understanding of God than he is usually credited with when he said that he could only believe in a dancing God. It is, he said, the devil that is serious and it is the spirit of gravity that causes all things to fall. So what does one do? "Not by wrath does one kill, but by laughing. Up, let us kill the spirit of gravity!"[7] It is tragic if Nietzsche, along with others, could not see Christianity doing this. Jesus emphasized the need for adults to learn from children: "I praise you, Father, Lord of heaven and earth, because you have hidden these things from the wise and learned, and revealed them to little children . . . truly I tell you, anyone who will not receive the kingdom of God like a little child will never enter it." True childishness, play and laughter are essential parts of an authentic spiritual life.

Living "As If . . ."

Living in the kingdom of God is very much like playing a game, in that it involves living or playing in a different world to the one that is otherwise inhabited. Every game, like the kingdom of God, creates its own world, a different reality with its own rules and environment, and in order to play that game, or live in that kingdom, one has to live by the rules. This means, for example, accepting that in chess a pawn may only move in a certain way, and in games of make-believe it means believing that a small patch of ground under a tree is really a kitchen, or that a table is a pirate ship and that sticks are really swords. Similarly, there is a sense in which Christians play a game when they live "as if" the invisible God really exists, "as if" Jesus had actually saved the world, and "as if" the Holy Spirit's presence is as real as that of the person standing next to them. This form of playing is a way of bringing a new reality into the present. Indeed, child psychologists will affirm the importance of make-believe for enabling children to become adults who are able to creatively conceive of and bring about new realities that previously only existed in their minds. Although Christians live within the present reality of the world they are also able to conceive and actualize

7. Nietzsche, *Thus Spoke Zarathustra*, 29.

a new and different reality as part of the kingdom of God, as citizens of heaven and possessors of eternal life.

Seeking to live out the life of the future kingdom of God in the present and living "as if" something is true is not only something that children do. It is a process that has long been used in psychotherapy, at least since the publication of *Man's Search for Meaning*, in which the prominent psychotherapist Viktor Frankl argued that meaning could be found in the midst of suffering by living "as if"—living in the way that one wants to be and to live, rather than being bound by repeating the way that one has been in the past. Similarly, in the philosophical world Hans Vaihinger wrote *The Philosophy of "As-If"* in which he argued that everyone lives by certain beliefs that they have invented, that they live by and that they project into the world to bring meaning and order to life.[8] These philosophical and psychological extensions of childhood play are helpful techniques for changing the way life is lived and creating a new reality.

This playfulness is analogous to the way that Christian seek to create the kingdom in the present, but Christians play and live "as if" with an intensity that extends even further. Christians believe that this alternate reality actually *is* present and is not merely an imagining or a future possibility. Children, despite having the ability to resolutely ignore the presence of adults or others who see their game as an illusion, are, at least usually, aware of the distinction between the game and reality and they are able to pause one and switch to the other and then back again. But Christians actually believe that the game that they are playing is the real truth, a genuine reality that does exist through the presence of the Spirit and in playing, praying, worshipping, ministry and service they contribute towards making it real. In ordinary play the players require a level of commitment to believing and acting in accordance with the rules and the environment of the world that is being created. This commitment is a form or a replica of faith, but in Christian play the believers have a definite faith that God is really at work in the world and their make-believe is actually making real the kingdom of God in the present. Faith, in the characteristic biblical construction of words, is not merely faith "in" (*ev*) certain things (as when one accepts the truth of a certain statement) but faith "into" (*pisteuō eis*) a new reality. It is a trust, a commitment that is like "faithing into" a new relationship with God and a new and exciting form of life. In this way Christian play is the most adventurous form of play. It involves testing one's abilities, exploring

8. Vaihinger, *Philosophy of "As-If"*.

new areas, pushing existing boundaries and making the mundane more exciting. "Advent" (or "a coming") is a term used with reference to both the first and second comings of Christ, but, as the term itself implies, it refers to not just any ordinary arrival but to an *advent*ure that is remarkable and exciting, a new form of play.

Playing with the Idea of Play

Playing and Learning with Children

This chapter suggests that adults can learn a lot spiritually from children, so go and observe some children play and see what you can learn from them about relating to God. Then make sure that you actually play with some children and ask the same question again. Then share your thoughts with someone else.

3

Worship: Fun and Games

Christ plays in ten thousand places.

—Gerard Manly Hopkins

We can't go any further in this exploration of play without playing a game of "What am I?" This is a riddle and you are to try and work out what the *two* activities are that *both* fit all of the following characteristics. Okay? Here are the clues: These two activities are both purely voluntary activities; people only ever do them because they want to. They both occur at their own specific times and in specific places, and they are subject to their own set of sometimes quite complex rules. These activities are fictitious in that they copy life in the "real world" without being exactly the same. Even when a lot of planning and practice take place the outcome of these activities can never be predicted (and if it could, they would be ruined). Some might regret the fact that both of these activities could be considered completely useless and unproductive activities in the sense that they do not create goods or wealth or, indeed, anything else. Consequently, it is not unusual for them to be perceived as a waste of time. Finally, despite the careful planning that often takes place, forms of these activities can spontaneously break out in just about anyway and at any time.[1]

You probably worked out, given the general theme of the book, that these are the characteristics of playing a game. But did you work out that all

---

1. A list of characteristics presented in a more formal way would indicate that play is (1) voluntary, (2) location and time specific, (3) controlled, (4) imitative, (5) unpredictable, (6) unproductive, and (7) spontaneous. This is discussed further in chapter 5, or see, for example, the works referred to in the bibliography by Johan Huizinga, Stuart Brown, and Brian Sutton-Smith.

26

of these criteria also fit worship as well as play? It is easy to see that games, or playing, function in this way, whether it is a riddle or chess or make-believe. Everyone playing knows that they are playing and only does so because they want to. They are aware of the rules (even if they cheat!) and of the boundaries of the game, and no one knows the outcome because there would be little point if one did. Neither a game of chess nor of make-believe really works if one knows in advance what is going to happen! The same is true of worship. Like play, it is an activity that is necessarily voluntary. Of course, there are some situations where people may be required to attend services, but actual worship only takes place when someone willingly engages in it. Worship, like play, is "fictitious" in that it copies life in the "real world" with symbolic eating and drinking and washing, with dress-ups and special actions and movements and songs, and yet it is not exactly the same; it has its own unique form and meaning. And, importantly, just as the final result of a game cannot be predicted nor can the outcome of worship. At least, that should be the case. God is a participant in, and not merely a recipient of, worship and God's actions with his people cannot be predicted! The outcome is inner and personal in the sense that it changes people's lives; it is not productive in any sense that a disinterested observer can discern. As with play there are many, many varieties of worship and it can take place anywhere, anytime. Finally, and perhaps most importantly, this activity is one that might to be undertaken simply for the joy of being able to participate in it.

Worship as Play

In 1918, in his book *The Spirit of the Liturgy*, Romano Guardini suggested—quite remarkably given the time of writing—that liturgy is like play. Worship is a time when one is like a child playing, not aiming at anything, with no purpose other than the pleasure of the game. It is an expression of life itself.[2] Linguistically, the term "liturgy" comes from the Greek *leitourgos*, which is compounded from *leitos*, meaning "of the people," and *ergon*, referring to "work." It originally referred, in ancient times, to doing public work such as mending a road or participating in local government at one's own expense. In the Septuagint, the second-century B.C. Greek translation of the Old Testament, it was used of the priests and Levites who "worked" at worship in the temple. It is rarely used in the New Testament

2. Guardini, *Spirit of the Liturgy*, 37–45.

but when it appears it refers to those who worship and pray. As a result of this background those who like etymological interpretations of words often describe worship as "the work of the people of God." Unfortunately, meanings based primarily on word origin alone, rather than context and usage, are rarely very accurate and in reality there is no linguistic argument for interpreting Christian worship literally in terms of the "work" of the people of God. But it is perhaps not really surprising that there is a tendency to relate worship to work (and thus to the closely associated concepts of productivity and efficiency) because of the prominent role that work has in Western society generally and within the church particularly. The Protestant work ethic and its related concepts, such as duty, responsibility, service, commitment and productiveness, emerged from within the life and theology of the Western church and they continue to influence both society and church life and worship. More will be said about this later but at this point it is sufficient to note that work, efficiency and productivity seem, to the Western mind, so normal and positive, as fundamentals of life, that it is completely natural to interpret worship in these terms: as an action that produces some measurable, spiritual effect.

As a result of this, corporate worship can very quickly be laden down with many responsibilities that it is expected to fulfill. Worship becomes the time to educate the people of God, as well as the focus of fellowship; it is often seen as the best time to inspire and encourage believers, as well as being the time for calling people to work for justice. It may also be a time for healing and answered prayer, and it often is expected to fulfill the function of evangelical outreach to those who are not yet believers. It is assessed and measured by the extent to which it does these things and by the time that it takes to do them.

In these various ways worship can be overloaded when, in reality, just like play, worship exists purely for its own sake and is not justified by some other end. Not even by good and worthy ends. Play only occurs because someone *wants* to play. One might go through the motions of a game, sport or play for some other reason—perhaps to keep someone happy or, like professional sportspeople, for money—but then it is not really play but a duty or work. Play is undertaken for pleasure alone. Play is its own reason for being and external motives inevitably detract from the joy of playing. It is the same with worship, where not even the best other purposes, such as healing, evangelism, teaching and mission, are needed to justify it. As with play, *worship itself* is the reason for worship, and external motives will inevitably detract from its intrinsic purpose.

The comparison of worship with play thus helps us overcome the typically Western, utilitarian way of thinking about worship as a means of producing or achieving something else and, beyond that, it also provides a model of what worship actually is—*a playful relationship with God.* Just as one could say that every form of play is an attempt to transcend the routine, ordinary life we live by inventing, often in great detail, another world with its own ways of being, so too one can say that every form of worship is an attempt to take the participant into the kingdom of God with its own distinctive way of life. Both play and worship can occur at particular, pre-arranged times that have been set apart for them, but they can also, of course, take place at absolutely any time at all. Some would reckon that spontaneous play is best of all, and some people have such a playful attitude to life that playfulness is with them all the time. Their playfulness is not found so much in specific activities that they engage in from time to time, as much as in an *attitude* of mind that produces a playful approach to the whole of life. Those who have this ability to find the playful dimension in all aspects of life find it enriched. To be able to find the creative, playful dimension of work, friendships, family relationships, community service and so forth is a real blessing. Worship is not only like this in that it can also take place at any time; it is also something that can become a life attitude. It is a great blessing to have a worshipful attitude to life so that God's kingdom can break into the world at any time.

Too often it seems that the present Christian life is about grace deferred. That is, the present life is a time to be endured rather than enjoyed as we await the glorious future kingdom of God. The present era is, indeed, a time that mixes joy and sorrow, pain and pleasure, tragedy and triumph, and we do await the final revelation of Christ in his glory, but the certainty of a future hope has implications for our understanding of the present time, for the kingdom is present as well as future and the glory of God is revealed all around us at this very moment.

So often this life is interpreted as a time of work and achievement that precedes a future rest, but while it is important to live productive lives that express a commitment to service of God and the world, one can question whether this life is primarily about achievement and things done. As Jürgen Moltmann says, the moments of this life that abide in eternity are found in the moments of grace and faith, joy and love, "not in the moments of glory due to achievements and efforts."[3] As much as this world is a preparation for the next it is also present demonstration of that life of play, dance, music, joy, and rejoicing. The biblical images of life in the eternal kingdom of God are not ones that stress or glorify human achievement; instead they focus on childlike play and joy, and we are able to experience a foretaste of the future eschatological life as we share in this playful joy in the present.

This is famously expressed in the Westminster Shorter Catechism, which asks, "What is the chief end of man?" And the answer is, "Man's chief end is to glorify God, and to enjoy him forever." The enjoyment of God is not something only for the future. It is for the present as well. This is expressed in the way that King David danced and played before the Lord (2 Sam 6:12–16). This appeared to be irreverent to others but not to the Lord. And when rebuked David insisted upon celebrating and being "undignified" in this way. Since at least the sixth century this has been expressed in Christian art in terms of a resurrection dance. Christ is, as Hippolytus of Rome (c.170–235) said, "the lead dancer in the mystical round" and the church is his "bride who dances along."[4] More recently the idea has been picked up by massed, public resurrection dances. It began on Easter Sunday when three hundred young people from Faith Church in Budapest took part in an enthusiastic resurrection dance in Victory Square and, apart from it becoming a YouTube hit, the next year Christians in sixty-five cities did the same. This kind of joyful, playful, dance, which is an expression of life with God, ought to be characteristic of the life of the believer. Life is misunderstood if it is only seen in terms of working for God; it is important to learn to play with God as well. Obedience and duty, sacrifice, service and self-giving need to be complemented with play and pleasure, joy and appreciation. In so doing the emphasis shifts from service of God to relationship with God.

Of course, one cannot ignore the pain and suffering of life, and more needs to be said about this later, but for the present it will have to be enough to observe that tragedy, pain and trauma are not overcome in this world by eliminating them (that is for the future kingdom, where there will be no more pain or suffering) but by finding God and divine joy in the midst of them. There is no place in life where Christ is not present and active or, as the poet Gerard Manley Hopkins expressed it in his poem "As Kingfishers

---

3. Moltmann, *Theology of Play*, 35.
4. Ibid., 36.

Catch Fire": "Christ plays in ten thousand places."[5] The poem is very well known but worth noting here. It really should be read aloud in order to hear the rhythm and the full sound of the expressive words.

> As kingfishers catch fire, dragonflies drāw flāme;
> As tumbled over rim in roundy wells
> Stones ring; like each tucked string tells, each hung bell's
> Bow swung finds tongue to fling out broad its name;
> Each mortal thing does one thing and the same:
> Deals out that being indoors each one dwells;
> Selves—goes itself; myself it speaks and spells,
> Crying Whāt I do is me: for that I came.
>
> Í say mōre: the just man justices;
> Kēeps grace: thāt keeps all his goings graces;
> Acts in God's eye what in God's eye he is—
> Christ—for Christ plays in ten thousand places,
> Lovely in limbs, and lovely in eyes not his
> To the Father through the features of men's faces.

Hopkins is stressing the point that everything naturally expresses its purpose: the colorful kingfisher "catches fire" and the dragonfly "draws flame" as they fly about, and stones ring when tossed into wells. Every mortal thing naturally does what it is made to do—express its inner essence, that which "indoors each one dwells" is compelled to express itself in life. Similarly, people express their true nature as they do justice, "keep grace" and act out God's special purposes. In doing this each person "is Christ" for Christ actually dwells "indoors" each one, and is revealed to the Father through the features of their faces—the way that they live and express their nature. In this way, through human life "Christ plays in ten thousand places." Christ engages in a dynamic interplay that will reflect the character of Christ in our lives.

The Different Games We Play

If we are to pursue the notion of worship as a form of play then one might ask, "What kind of game is it that we are playing in worship?" because, as

---

5. In Hopkins, *Poems of Gerard Manly Hopkins*, 54.

we have already noted, there are so many different kinds of play. Are we to compare worship with card games, word games, or physical games? Or perhaps worship is more like a role-playing game or a game of pretend and make-believe? Is worship like a board game or a computer game? Or mayby it's more of a puzzle? Hopefully it is not like a war game! Any analogy can be pushed too far and turned into an absurdity, but there are good biblical reasons for comparing worship to certain forms of playfulness and the reality is that there are different traditions that play different worship games.

Playing with the Mind

Some people prefer *mind games* such as chess or a crossword puzzle and there are forms of worship that focus upon the mind as well. These are services of worship that typically have lots of words, ideas and concepts in them. Sometimes the focus is on the words of the actual liturgy while at other times the intellectual focus is the sermon, but whether there is a liturgical focus or a homiletic one the point is that the mind is always engaged. A strong, mentally demanding liturgical focus occurs in any full Orthodox service. Surprisingly, I found that my experiences of participation in Orthodox services in languages I did *not* know (including Armenian, Russian and Greek) were actually a good deal easier than participating in an English Orthodox liturgy. When one does not understand the languages one inevitably focuses upon the visual elements of the service without having to pay attention to what is being said. But a service spoken and sung at a rapid rate in English over three and a half hours is more challenging—theologically powerful, conceptually rich and intellectually challenging compared with many other forms of service—providing that one gives one's attention to it. The liturgy is the action of the church in coming together to worship, to pray, to sing, to hear God's Word and to be instructed in God's commandments. It is an all-inclusive act of prayer, worship, teaching and the communion of the whole church in heaven and on earth. It is not merely prayer, nor one of the sacraments; it is the one sacramental manifestation of the church as the community of God. The length and complexity of the service is somewhat offset by the repetition that takes place, as the same structure is used each week, nonetheless this is a service that is unapologetic about the intellectual demands it places on the worshipper.

In other places it is the sermon that provides the intellectual challenge. Such sermons will tend to be long rather than short and will, of course, typically revolve around Scripture in order; as the collect of the Book of Common Prayer says, the people will "read, mark, learn and inwardly digest" the meaning and the implications of the biblical text. The sermon not only expounds the teaching of Scripture but also finds its justification for doing so within Scripture itself as it takes seriously the words of the Lord to Joshua, "keep this Book of the Law always on your lips; meditate on it day and night, so that you may be careful to do everything written in it" (Josh 1:8). By focusing on Scripture in this way the believer will resist being "conformed to the pattern of this world" and will be "transformed by the renewing of your mind," to "know the truth" that sets one free (Rom 12:2; Eph 4:23; John 8:32). A playful approach to serious biblical teaching will influence the entire approach a preacher takes and will do more than provide a humorous title; nonetheless, I am tempted to note, with playful and serious intent, my candidates for "The Top Ten Sermons That Need to Be Preached." They are:

1. A DIY Guide to Justification

2. How to Meditate in 60 Seconds

3. The Dummies' Guide to Wisdom

4. How to Be Holy without Really Trying

5. The Seven Essential Habits of Biblical Numerologists

6. Discipleship Made Easy

7. Everything There Is to Know about God

8. The Rough Guide to Heaven

9. The Lonely Planet Guide to Hell

10. How to Get What You Want Out of Worship

11. A Beginners' Guide to Entire Sanctification.[6]

---

6. Yes, I know there are eleven, but whoever put out a list of "The Top Eleven" of anything?

Playing with the Body

There are others who prefer more physical play where the pleasure does not come from mental illumination but from physical movement. There are several forms of play, including the pleasure of simple physical exertion (as there is in exercise and running), the development of physical skills (as in tennis or gymnastics) and the experience of vertigo and disorientation, as when young children giggle when they are tossed into the air and are caught again and when older children want to be whirled around in circles. Adults also find a curious pleasure in experiencing the giddiness, and sometimes the terror, that comes from fairground and theme-park rides. One might begin with the lights, music and gentle movement of a merry-go-round and, over the years, work up to the more extreme roller coaster or even the explosive vertical thrust into the air and then the sudden plunge of the Tower of Terror.

There are services of worship that reflect these various physical experiences and they are found in different traditions from liturgical to Pentecostal. Of course, some people prefer relatively physically passive worship, but for others the active use of the body is important. It can involve movements as simple as kneeling to pray, making the sign of the cross, becoming prostrate or swaying to music. These both reflect and affect the spiritual attitude that one has or that one seeks in worship. But the movement can also be much more exuberant movement. Liturgical dance sometimes involves a well-rehearsed performance by a few but there is also the case of the Shakers, an eighteenth-century community that used dance as the basis of their worship for the whole congregation with intricate routines expressing various aspects of their faith. Just as some people revel in the less controlled aspects of physical movement so too can worshippers, with some congregations preferring their dance to come through a more personal expression of whatever movement seems appropriate to the individual. Those who appreciate the physicality involved in worship are typically fond of reminding others that king David danced "with all his might" before God (2 Sam 6:14). One might also remember that in so doing some people were offended, but not God.

While some forms of dance and creative movement are carefully planned and choreographed, there are also times in worship when there is a loss of control in movement as people fall over in response to the movement of the Spirit or move ecstatically with feelings akin to that of vertigo. There can be moments of disorientation in physical movement as much as there can be in the mental life moments of cognitive dissonance as people are challenged to move to new and perhaps more radical forms of discipleship. The focused attention given to worship can mean reduced external awareness and perhaps visions or heightened emotions, and sometimes feelings of euphoria. There are those who are suspicious of such unusual, mystical or ecstatic experiences and it is important to be wary of two extremes in this regard. On the one hand one ought to avoid the confusion of feeling with grace—it cannot be assumed that all unusual feelings or experiences are necessarily a special revelation of divine blessing. Moreover, when particular experiences do occur it is, as the apostle Paul argued, a conceit to assume a superiority for spectacular experience over rational expressions of faith (1 Cor 12). On the other hand, one cannot simply exclude the physical, the experiential or the ecstatic from the realm of divine activity in human life. God plays in us in many ways. Paul himself experienced visions and revelations and "was caught up to the third heaven. Whether it was in the body or out of the body I do not know" (2 Cor 12:1–2), and there are, of course, other biblical accounts of visions and dreams. This reminds us of the wholeness of the person in worship, with body and spirit an integrated an interactive whole. Physical posture and movement interact with one's mental and spiritual state; worship is not merely a passive experience and not purely a mental or rational endeavor. It is by no means irrational but it can lie beyond simple rationality and take one into the presence of God, as Charles Wesley expressed it, "lost in wonder, love and praise."[7]

Playing with the Imagination

Worship that takes us beyond normal experience is a reminder that we are engaged in a playful relationship with God and that there is a sense in which God is playing with us. Worship like this may involve a form of disorientation not completely unlike what one experiences in some forms of physical play, but this is not surprising as one's sense of the world is being changed through it. Worship is a form of play that can, and should, provide surprising experiences. It may disorient us in order to reorient us and reveal to us new ways of living. In thinking of the presence of the kingdom it may, however, be a mistake to focus solely, or even especially, on ecstatic experience. Reflecting on the use of the imagination in worship, as in play, is as important as

7. From his hymn "Love Divine, All Love Excelling." Quoted from Watson, ed., *Annotated Anthology of Hymns.*

thinking about play and worship of the mind and the body, because it enables us to imagine the future kingdom of God in the present.

The imagination develops at a very early age as children pretend that things are not exactly as they seem to be. They imagine themselves to be in other places or to be invisible and they pretend to be other people. They love to dress up and use their imagination to become a mother or a father, a fireman or a teacher or perhaps an astronaut or a super hero. The imagination is also, of course, used by older children, teens and adults in ever more complex way—in simple board games, in playing charades, in engaging in complex virtual reality games, and in appreciating movies and, of course, "plays." In all of these games alternate forms of life are acted out with apparently infinite variation.

When the imagination is used in a parallel manner in worship it enables us to see ways in which God can work in the present. For the believer, of course, the world created in worship is not an imaginary world but the most real of all possible worlds—one that is, in fact, more real and true than the present world. This is theologically so because faith is a form of imagination, because to have faith means that one is living as though it is true that Jesus is Lord, that salvation has been won and that the kingdom is both present and future. Faith is not merely a form of assent to certain doctrines; it is much more a form of trusting, or actually living in, a new reality that God has made. There is a sense in which faith is a form of make-believe: it means living as though everything that God says is true and has come about. In worship one acts *as if* it were true, but with the belief that it *really is* so. Imagination is central to faith and a playful attitude lies at the heart of worship, and it is these capacities that enable the believer to transcend the immediate world and experience the new. Play and imagination are central to religious experience.

Some traditions utilize the imagination extensively. The Orthodox liturgy, for example, dramatically re-presents, through word, action, color, light, symbol and smell, the whole drama of salvation from the time before creation (represented by the preparations that take place behind the icon screen) through to the final consummation of all things. The vestments, icons, processions, movements, words and songs are all designed to make the liturgy become heaven on earth. Everything possible is done to enable worshippers to experience this as a reality. It is a rich experience that is played out each time the liturgy is performed, one into which people immerse themselves. It is not enough to be an observer of worship; both play and worship require active participation. The presentation of the story of salvation through the liturgy is not intended as a representation of something that will happen in the future, or of something that has happened elsewhere. It intends to communicate that this is the reality for the present, for *this* world. It is this world that has been redeemed and worship shows us how to perceive it now.

Although some traditions emphasize the use of the imagination in worship more than others almost all Christians use it in the celebration of the Lord's Supper. It may be known variously as Eucharist, Mass or Holy Communion and celebrated in different ways but through the use of bread and wine, word, action, symbol and color this worship re-creates another world. The bread and wine will never be enough to feed someone physically; instead it is a representation of a spiritual feeding. And in the act of gathering together and sharing in eating and drinking there is a belief that the communicants are *actually* meeting with Christ and the whole "communion of saints." To outsiders it may seem that the worshippers are pretending that the kingdom is present, just as children pretend that a small patch of ground is a deserted island or that a garden shed is a castle, but believers see it as really true.

They believe, as an act of faith, that Jesus *is* Lord despite the circumstances that exist in the world, that death *has* been conquered, that the kingdom of God *is* among us and that as they eat and drink Christ is actually present. In theological terms there are debates about the way in which this presence is "real" and there are, indeed, some who do not see it that way at all, but for the others the real presence of Christ is at the heart of a new playful imagining of the world.

The Play Life of Churches

One observer of the play life of churches, James H. Evans, suggests that many traditional churches have lost their corporate playfulness in worship because they have come to misunderstand the nature of participation in worship and have turned worship from a game to a task.

> One could say the traditional churches have focused on participation in the life of the congregation, but that participation has gradually lost it ludic character, quickly becoming mere labor or tasks . . . Mega churches have focused on the spectacle of worship,

but that spectacle has lost its ludic character . . . It is easy for members of these churches to feel like detached spectators.[8]

In contemporary life we are all well adapted to being spectators or "private participants." Theater, film, television and video have taught us to consume entertainment and to be satisfied with a purely internal response to the drama, the humor, the pathos, the excitement, the despair or whatever emotion is placed before us. It is easy to engage in worship in the same way. It is, indeed, a form of engagement and it is worship and it is meaningful, but it is minimally ludic when there is little or no possibility of the participants becoming active players who can give direction to where the worship is going, interact with other participants or directly respond to those who are leading.

In some Orthodox and Catholic (and occasionally Protestant) traditions the time immediately after Easter (either the week or the following Sunday) has been a "play day" or "Bright Sunday," a time for joy and laughter that was (and sometimes still is) celebrated variously with parties, picnics, practical jokes, singing, dancing and sermons with jokes in them. The point is to celebrate the resurrection of Jesus in a more exuberant way than the liturgical practices of most traditions usually allow. (Which reminds me of a joke. A very enthusiastic and outgoing worshipper used to informal worship services visited a very formal and restrained service in another church. During the sermon he was excited by the preaching and spontaneously yelled out, "Praise the Lord!" A man sitting nearby leaned across and whispered, "Excuse me," he said, "we don't 'Praise the Lord!' here." At which point another regular worshipper said, "Oh yes we do. It's on page 47.")

It is sometimes argued that the practical jokes of Bright Sunday and Monday reflect the view expressed by some early church theologians that at Easter the devil was fooled by God. Gregory of Nyssa, for example, extended the ancient imagery of Christ's death as a ransom in such a way that God is seen as deliberately tricking the devil. That is, Christ is offered as a ransom in exchange for humanity and the devil thinks he has a good bargain. But God hid Christ's divinity under his human nature, which meant that he was too powerful for the devil and so was able to be rescued from the devil's hold and raised from death. A somewhat different version is found in Augustine and, later, in Peter Lombard to the effect that the cross was a mousetrap baited with the blood of Christ. Once again the devil is

8. Evans, *Playing*, 78.

fooled and the righteous laugh (except for those who find the imagery of the mousetrap a little uncomfortable). With or without those particular images the *risus paschalis*—the "Easter laugh," as the early theologians called it—should sound out down through the ages because the resurrection of Christ ought to be a matter of great joy whether or not it is formally instituted into the liturgy of the church. One Catholic version of this tradition that originated in Bavaria in the fifteenth century involved the priests inserting funny stories into their sermons and scathing descriptions of the devils' vain attempts to keep the doors of hell locked against Christ who came to free the devil's captives. But, in the opinion of some at least, it got a little out of hand and led to some rather curious interpretations of Scripture and the practice was banned in the seventeenth century by Clement X and in the eighteenth by Maximilian III and the bishops of Bavaria.[9] In medieval France at Auxerre in the twelfth century Easter worship involved a decorated church, the bishop dancing and ball games for all. The dean would carry a ball in the procession into the sanctuary and on reaching the altar would also dance. There is a ritual for vespers from Besancon dating from 1528 that includes dancing and the distribution of wine. This was held on or around New Year's Day. At around the same time in Vitre on the Feast of St. Stephen there was a custom of elevating a ball that had been placed on the altar for that purpose, during the Mass, between the elevation of the chalice and the host.[10] However, in most places there has been a constant struggle between those who want to affirm the theological and liturgical use of laughter and those who see it as inappropriate. Many practices and traditions have been suppressed either permanently or for awhile.

More recently a "Holy Humor Sunday" movement has taken place among some churches. The idea is that Christians should "shout for joy to the Lord" (Ps 98:4) and it involves a wide variety of ways of holding holy humor worship services. These usually take place on the Sunday following Easter, and many congregations have found that what was previously a "low Sunday," following the high of the previous week, has become a popular and well-attended service. It reminds people not only of the ongoing joy of the resurrection but also of the fact that God delights in laughter and is the one who created our sense of humor. It demonstrates to church members a particular way of expressing faith in God, and a service of fun has been known to bring healing to a fractious congregation. Laughter

9. Herbermann, *Catholic Encyclopedia*, "Easter."

10. Rahner, *Man at Play*, 78–87.

and joy is a form of healing for the despondent and therapy for those who are suffering hard times. It has also been used to introduce sensitive topics ("the funny side of aging").

Services focusing on holy humor and laughter can also be associated with the use of color, flowers, balloons and dressing up. There are many songs and hymns of joy that suit such occasions and prayers and liturgies that express joy and laughter ought to come to the fore. It seems that many liturgical resources are written by very serious people, when corporate expressions of worship ought to express a joy-filled, even playful or humorous life much of the time, perhaps even a foolishness according to standards of the world.

Worship as Fun

This leads us to the final, rather obvious lesson from the analogy between play and worship. It is that worship ought to be . . . well, I almost hesitate to say it . . . but it ought to be *fun*. And the reason for the hesitation is that it is likely to be misunderstood on several counts. So let me make a quick preliminary defense of the idea. Firstly, it doesn't mean that worship is to be trivialized or turned into entertainment. True fun—incorporating joy and happiness—does not have to be trivial or simply entertainment. And secondly this claim doesn't mean that worship does not include sadness and grief, somberness and solemnity, anger and despair. Not at all, but the believer's fundamental joy in the presence of Christ and the knowledge of the kingdom of God, which in worship is made real in the present, is not displaced by an awareness of the tragedies of this world. The sadnesses that are inevitably felt by everyone are undeniable and find their place in worship, but they are also embraced and given meaning by the actual presence of the future and the ultimate resolution of all things, which is the gift given to us in Christ and the presence of his kingdom.

Meeting with God is always a serious and can be a challenging business. This has already been shown in the previous discussion about wrestling with God—a form of play that involves real contest. But everything in life that is brought into worship—including, as happens very appropriately, the difficulties and traumas of life—ought to be seen within the context of the world having been redeemed by Christ and the worship life of the church being a present participation in the life of the future kingdom of God. Everything should be seen and understood on this basis. This does not mean ignoring them, but nor can they completely displace the joy of salvation and the knowledge of the future.

In saying that worship is fun it should be clear that the fun described here is not trivial but a recognition of the joy that should underpin the life of every believer. This is not the kind of fun that comes from being entertained, although there are those who argue that if worship is to reflect an underlying joy in the Lord that it is not inappropriate to express it in that way. And pastors, worship leaders and preachers can all feel the weight of expectation in regard to worship when people compare what happens in church with the very dominant cultural forms of public presentation in movies and on television. The search for liturgies and forms of worship that reflect the quality and the forms, the entertainment and fun of other public events can lead to the focus falling on style rather than substance.

In an inevitable reaction to this there are those who stress that worship must be removed from any thought of fun or entertainment, in order to distinguish it from other activities and to enable a stress on the fact that worship is not for us but is what we do for God. The responsibility of worshippers is to offer praise, thanksgiving, prayers and the thoughts and desires of one's heart to God in gratitude for divine grace. Now obviously there is a point in what is being asserted here—that worship is not entertainment—but it is also necessary to say that the view that worship is what we do for God is also unhelpful. Indeed, both approaches are mistaken because neither is sufficiently playful. One stresses what one receives in worship while the other stresses what one does, but neither stresses sufficiently the level of engagement that is intrinsic to authentic Trinitarian worship and is analogous to the participatory nature of children playing together.

On the one hand, play is fun and enjoyable but not in the same way that a performance is fun and entertaining. One observes a performance. Entertainment is provided. But one has to *engage* in play. On the other hand, it does not do justice to worship to envisage it simply as an offering of praise and thanks from believers to God. It too is insufficiently playful" and insufficiently Trinitarian as well. Indeed, both these views have what is an essentially unitarian view of worship that lacks the participatory dimension of Trinitarian worship and turns the emphasis away from play towards worship as work.[11]

This approach is unitarian because pastor, priest and people are on one side, offering worship to God, who is on the other side, hearing the

11. Torrance, *Worship, Community, and the Triune God of Grace*, 9.

prayer and receiving the worship. But Trinitarian worship is the gift of participating through the Spirit in the incarnate Son's communion with the Father. Worship is nothing less than fellowship (participating or sharing) in the very life of God. The believer's life is embraced *within the life of God*. This is union with God. There is no sense either of simply being a recipient of what God (or the pastor) offers or of being one whose sole responsibility is to offer praise to God. While the notion of worship as a dialogue where there is a movement back and forth comes closer to the mark this still does not fully encapsulate the level of engagement represented by children playing together.

To say that we play with God is a way of exploring the deeply participatory experience that we have, which is new life *in Christ*, not external to, but *sharing in*, God's life. The joyfulness and the participatory nature of play makes it one of the best images for expressing the way that we are embraced within Trinitarian fellowship. It is not surprising that the prophet Zechariah's description of the heavenly Jerusalem includes the city being filled "with boys and girls playing there" (Zech 8:3). Worship brings this future life into the present.

Playing with the Idea of Play

Playing in Worship

There are many ways of "playing" worship, identify the kind of "game" that your church plays and the kind of playing that you prefer. Visit a church that plays in a different way and try and really participate in it. Are there aspects of play that your church community could benefit from? Perhaps discuss worship and play with someone you know who leads worship.

It is sometimes helpful to "play" with Scripture. Next time you read a passage of the Bible—especially a narrative section—try to imagine yourself as a part of the story. See yourself as being present, watching and listening, and pay attention to your response to what is taking place and the way you would want to be involved.

4

Spirituality: Playing with Friends

Play is at the foundation of all personal relationships.

—STUART BROWN

After decades of research into play Stuart Brown accumulated a huge catalog of play's effects summarized in his book *Play: How It Shapes the Brain, Opens the Imagination, and Invigorates the Soul.* Perhaps most importantly of all, he shows how play creates a foundation for all personal relationships.[1] In doing this he also implicitly shows that the accumulated research on human play provides a confirmation of the theological tradition that associates play with the human-divine relationship, including, for example, Thomas Aquinas's insights regarding the importance of the connection between play and contemplative prayer—the most intimate relationship one can have with God.[2]

One is able to see the way that play creates the foundation for personal relationships by looking at research on the very first personal relationship— between mother and child. Research in the 1960s showed that babies do better, in terms of brain development and thus in terms of emotional and intellectual adjustment, with enriched environments that includes toys, color, movement and so forth. (The initial research was actually done with rats rather than human babies but it was assumed that the results would transfer to humans and that seems to be right.) Parents now are well aware of this developmental issue and so children today are much more likely to be given a rich environment of toys and books with visual and tactile

---

1. Brown, *Play*, 13.

2. As discussed in chapter 1.

stimulation. But, interestingly, it is not really the toys as such that are the issue; they are simply the medium by which the child and the parents can develop a richer, more playful relationship. It is the relationship that provides the real foundation for so many aspects of later life. The key lies in an *enriched relationship* rather than just an enriched environment. Enhancing the environment for a solitary rat (or child) does not make any difference; it is the interaction that is important.

In play one is learning about other people and relationships; play is essential for developing love, trust, empathy, care, fairness, sharing and other positive characteristics. The intimacy of the interaction in this first relationship is seen in physical changes that are quite remarkable—the brain rhythms of mother (and often father) and child synchronize. At three or four months in normal, healthy circumstances, when a child and parent make eye contact they will typically smile at each other, the baby is likely to make little sounds, the mother may sing or speak or make noises and, as an EEG will show, the neural activity in the right cortex of their brains will synchronize. They experience a joyful union that is experienced physically and emotionally.

This neural attunement reflects the personal, emotional attachment that is commonly known as "bonding" and it is the most basic state of play, which is the foundation for more complex states of play and all personal relationships. Play is what attunes people with one another; it is critical for the development of emotional self-regulation and those who do not experience it tend to be more emotionally erratic and have difficulty forming healthy attachments. The development of the cortex, however, buffers the child against excessive surges of emotion. Play creates a state of attunement and brings people together in a manner analogous to the way in which those playing music together come into tune with each other.

The first relationship between parent and child is obviously critical but there is a sense in which in every game, and every form of play at every time, people come into tune with each other. This is obviously at the core of family and friend relationships, where playing together is a prominent characteristic of the relationship, but the beneficial effects of play in attunement are easily transferable and can be seen, for example, in an organizational context when workers play a game before a business meeting. In play one simply has to be involved; one usually finds pleasure and one learns how others interact so that, generally, people will get on better, including couples more romantically, if they play and explore new things together. Play is a means of cooperation and collaboration that heightens the enjoyment of life and makes space for creativity and innovation. Play allows one to learn from making mistakes in the attempt to pursue that which is new and different.

Relationships through Play

Play is developmentally important—emotionally, cognitively and socially—and there are also several ways that play is critically important spiritually. Firstly, play creates a capacity for relationship that is essential for a healthy spiritual relationship. Without the ability to engage in healthy, interactive relationships with other people one will inevitably struggle in developing a healthy relationship with God. The saving grace in this is . . . nothing other than the saving grace of God! God has a particular love, a special mercy, for those who are "the poor" of the world. This particularly includes those who have difficulty making relationships. In biblical thought "the poor" is not so much an economic term as a reference to those who are socially or rela-tionally poor—the widowed, the orphaned, the alien in a foreign land, the socially rejected, the despised, the mentally and spiritually ill. The greatness of the gospel is that God loves those who have difficulty loving because they have not been loved themselves. Or one might say that God loves to play with those who have not had people who have played with them.

Secondly, play is not only spiritually important in a preparatory sense; ongoing play is also critical as a fundamental means of attunement with God. It is the way our brain rhythms (metaphorically), emotions, minds and souls (actually) become spiritually attuned or "at one." The English word "atonement" was specially created in the sixteenth century as "at-one-ment" in order to translate Hebrew and Greek words describing what God has done in dealing with the alienating effects of sin and bringing people into union with himself. It refers to being "at one" or being in harmony. Through the work of Christ and the presence of the Holy Spirit it is possible to be attuned with God. The New Testament speaks of this in terms of the "fellow-ship" or the "communion" of the Holy Spirit. This fellowship (*koinonia*) can be used in an everyday sense, as when it is said that Simon Peter, James and John shared in (or "had shares in") a boat and a fishing business. Sharing in (or "having shares in") the Holy Spirit does not mean anything other than that we share in the Spirit's life. We share "in God," or one can say "the Spirit of God lives in you" and, consequently, the fruit, or the characteristics of the Spirit, emerge as spiritual attunement takes place.[3] This is an intimate engagement with God, a participation in the divine life.

Play is a means of encounter extending from simple interactions to complex forms of relationship and it involves the capacity to respond creatively and adaptively to the other. God engages in a playful relationship with his people, engaging in such a way that the freedom, creativity and the integrity of each person is affirmed and enhanced. It is a relationship of love in which no player is completely passive and in which every player experiences great joy. This is the central thesis of this book—that play is the essential and ultimate form of relationship with God. A playful attitude, I suggest, lies at the very heart of all spirituality and is critical for the whole of life.

Every relationship has its own form, or forms, of relating that constitute the content of the relationship. Something needs to be happening or else, by definition, there is no relationship; that something can be characterized in a variety of ways, and play is the best way of characterizing our final relationship with God. Play is the form that praise, adoration, worship and participation in the divine life actually take. Speaking in the language of play has the advantage of emphasizing the joyfulness, the freedom, the dynamic interactivity and the friendship that is intrinsic to this attunement.

Characterizing the divine-human relationship as playful provides a contrast with other expressions of the relationship that are characterized more by work and outcomes than the fun and the apparent purposeless of play. There are several versions of this. (a) One alternate view with a different emphasis on the fundamental nature of our relationship with God is that of God as all-powerful sovereign who works for our good in rescuing his people and producing good outcomes through life and beyond. This is a view that stresses that God is for us. God is the one who works on our behalf and it emphasizes the sovereignty and control of God and divine strength in contrast with human weakness. (b) Another view that is very similar in the way that it still has a focus on work and outcomes rather than play is that which stresses the role of people as the servants of God. Here the emphasis shifts slightly so that it falls on the way that God is the one who enables and empowers his servant people to engage in ministry. This view stresses the point that God is with us. God is certainly still the one who has the power but this view emphasizes the cooperative way that God works with people. And the more that the cooperative dimension of the

3. See 2 Cor 13:14; Luke 5:10; Rom 8:9; Gal 5:22–23.

divine-human relationship is stressed the more the work becomes like play. And no longer is God only for us or with us but now the emphasis falls on the mysterious way that God is in us. God is so close that there is a union, a harmony or a state of attunement that is like the attunement that babies have when they play with their parents.

The relationship between mother and baby comes to the fore in considering the way in which play creates a capacity for healthy relationships but, as shown above, play is also critical in the ongoing development of relationships and in this regard friendship as an important form of relationship comes to center stage. Almost by definition friends play together. This may involve formal games and recognizable times of play or it may simply involve an informal playfulness but, whatever the form, playfulness is the expression of the mutual pleasure, the joy, the humor and the stimulation of interacting with one's friend. Play is important; friends play together in some way or else they cease to be friends. And playing with someone is an implicit declaration of friendship. Consequently, while it is important for Christians to understand the significance of the whole range of metaphors of God as Lord, King, Savior, Shepherd, Guide and so forth, the image of God as Friend in particularly important in consideration of play.

A connection with friendship is one of three primary characteristics of play. At the start of chapter 3 a riddle was included to provide a playful way of expounding on what could otherwise have just been a logical, academic listing of the formal characteristics of play, as others have previously developed in similar fashion. Such a listing typically includes noting that play involves a voluntary activity that occurs spontaneously at specific times and in particular places, and is subject to its own set of, sometimes quite complex, rules, and is fictitious in that it imitates life in the "real world" without being exactly the same. The outcome of this "unproductive" activity cannot be predicted and it is undertaken purely for its own sake. Now, with the introduction of the concept of friendship it is possible to characterize play in a very human way with the characteristics of play clustering around three broad dimensions that conveniently alliterate as "friendship," "freedom" and "fun"—with friendship as the key concept that unlocks the significance role that play plays, both in ordinary human play and sacred playing with God.

Friendship and Play

When Robert Johnston, author of *The Christian at Play*, looked for evidence of play specifically in the life of Jesus he found it primarily contained within the accounts of Jesus' various friendships and in his teaching about friendship. He observes that "one will look in vain for a fully developed theology of play in the New Testament"[4] (though it would be a superficial view of play if one expected to find literal descriptions of games or other playful activities). What is of greater significance is the attitude of playfulness that one finds in the open, engaging relationship that is shared among friends. This is the kind of relationship that Jesus had with people, so much so that some scornfully suggested that Jesus had become "a glutton and a drunkard, a friend of tax collectors and sinners" (Luke 7:34). And they were right in one sense—that Jesus engaged in joyful friendships.[5]

These friendships were clearly important to him and he deliberately contrasted his own way of life with the more ascetic approach of John the Baptist. He engaged in friendship not only with his disciples but, most explicitly, with those whom others rejected such as the woman who poured perfume on his feet, Zacchaeus, tax collectors and the woman of Samaria (Luke 7:38; 19:1; John 4:1). The best place in Scripture to see what the kingdom of heaven is like is to look at Jesus' own way of life. He exemplified the kingdom and those friendships that were scorned by the Pharisees can rightly be seen as an anticipation of the friendship, playfulness, joy and laughter of the new creation.

Those wedded to a strong work ethic, those who understand personal identity through work and any who see play as frivolous, secondary or lightweight may find it hard to accept that the claim that the kingdom is seen more in play than in work or ministry (just as Martha found it unfair when Mary took time out with Jesus) because it can, indeed, be hard to accept grace! Knowing Christ as Lord is essential but so too is knowing Christ as Friend—one with whom one can engage in play. Indeed, in Jesus' own teaching a mature relationship with his disciples involved them deliberately shifting away from the notion of servanthood to one of friendship. He told those who had followed him for some years and who had shared with him in many ways, "*I no longer call you servants*, because a servant does not know

---

4. Johnston, *Christian at Play*, 119.
5. Edgar, *God Is Friendship*, 53–56.

his master's business. Instead *I have called you friends*, for everything that I learned from my Father I have made known to you" (John 15:15).

Jesus' own thought moves from servanthood as an early stage of ministry to friendship as the more mature form of relationship. Unfortunately, all too often this development has been reversed. And perhaps this is not too surprising as it is very easy to unconsciously resist the simplicity of grace. It is as though the idea of friendship is preliminary to the more serious, mature notions of service and leadership, which are considered to be more appropriate for those further advanced in Christian life and ministry. But this is complete reversal of the biblical imagery. It is true that friendship is a good and easy concept with which to help a child begin a relationship with Jesus, but it is wrong to think that it is a concept that belongs primarily to children and it is a serious mistake to reverse the direction of Jesus' own thought and imply, in any way, that friendship is superseded by servanthood as a more appropriate and mature form of relationship for teenagers or adults. Indeed, Jesus' line of thought works in precisely the opposite direction. Friendship with Jesus is a more mature relationship than servanthood. The problem is that "friendship with God" can appear to be a view of discipleship that is too lightweight (when compared with the glorious sacrifices of servanthood), too ordinary a relationship to have with God in Christ (as it is the kind of relationship we have with many other people) and perhaps too arrogant a relationship to elevate over servanthood (given that greatest thing that can be said about God is the he is the Lord of the universe). But, as I have suggested, the greatest difficulty in accepting friendship as the basic form of relationship with God can be precisely the difficulty of accepting grace. To think of it as too simple or lightweight is to fall into a legalism that suggests that we are saved by the radical sacrifices of our discipleship. To think of friendship as too ordinary or unworthy for the unique relationship we ought to have with God is a failure to understand the depth of God's grace, as though the incarnation brought God near but not too close. To think of friendship with God as too great a relationship for mere human beings is to underestimate the extent of God's grace shown to us. One of our primary tasks in the Christian life is to overcome the temptation to revert to a works-based form of relationship with God and, instead, to seek to restore the concept of friendship to its rightful place as a primary definition of Christian life and ministry. This present book about play is, in fact, an almost inevitable development of my previous book,

God is Friendship: A Theology of Spirituality, Community, and Society, because it explores further exactly what it is that friends do together—they play. [6]

The implications for the mode of Christian life are significant. The concept of friendship has implications for the way that believers relate to others as well as to God. It is a very close, intimate, egalitarian relationship and it offers an intimacy that is not based on the expectations inherent in family relationships, but is grounded in the free act of one who chooses to embark on a journey of personal exploration. No model can express everything, and a friendship model may not be able to represent the more transcendent notions of awe, holiness, majesty or "the fear of the Lord" but it should take its place as a significant model for Christian life, ministry and mission.

Friendship also has many other advantages as a relational model. It is simple enough to be understood by everyone and yet it is also profound, with such depth of meaning that the implications deserve to be explored in detail. It is a universal image of the Christian life that can be applied to every Christian: not all are pastors or apostles and not everyone is a deacon, a bishop or an evangelist, but everyone can be a friend of God. Unlike many of the other images that describe the relationship of the believer to God (master-disciple, Father-son/daughter, Lord-servant) it is symmetrical in its reciprocity (friend-friend), something that introduces a new dimension to the whole relationship of believers with God. It is also a personal relationship, much more personal than the master-servant relationship. This image is of particular importance because Jesus himself gave it a priority and thus it is applicable to all. And, of course, friends play together.

At its deepest level friendship is a free, voluntary and non-utilitarian activity. Friends are those whose company brings pleasure and satisfaction. Where there has to be compulsion or other incentive to meet there is no real friendship—though that is not to say that friendship cannot develop in such circumstances, in which case compulsion will become unnecessary. In this free relationship there can be adventure, creativity and fun or, perhaps more formally, joy or pleasure. But while there is some point in the shift towards joy or pleasure, perhaps to avoid any sense of triviality found in mere fun, this ought not be taken as completely eliminating the simple joy of laughter and mutual amusement from the relationship of friends. This is an aspect of the relationship that is usually recognized as appropriate in terms of ordinary human relationships, but equally often downplayed

6. Ibid.

in terms of one's relationship with God which is typically regarded in a much more serious and dour fashion. It is, in fact, time to recover the joy of relationship with God that comes through play.

Competitive and Cooperative Play

One of the key elements of play—indeed for Johan Huizinga it is *the* key element—is the agonistic dimension. That is, some form of competition or contest is seen as central to the playing of games. Huizinga is "fervently convinced" of the underlying identity between play and contest and he develops this theme in his *Homo Ludens: A Study of the Play-Element in Culture*.[7] Some are not so convinced that it is *the* key element, not least because of the obvious influence of other elements such as the creative dimension, as when one "plays music," but nonetheless one needs to recognize the fundamental connection. Competition is misunderstood when it is only seen as setting people in opposition when it actually unites opposing players in a common enterprise. In the complex dynamic between competition and cooperation, awareness of the other is increased and friendship developed. But, of course, one needs to carefully observe the balance. Scottish tennis pro Andy Murray tells how, when they were quite young, he took his girlfriend, Kim, on a first date to Brighton Pier. Amongst other things, they played air hockey, and although he doesn't remember it Kim does because she thought he might be chivalrous and let her win a few points but he didn't let her win a single one. "I guess," a more mature Murray commented, "she might have realized then that I am a just wee bit competitive."[8] It is often reckoned that competition brings out the worst in people but I want to suggest that is really an aberration. With the right attitude competitions and contests are positive aspects of relationship that can enhance our abilities and our understanding of ourselves and God. It is also sometimes said that "cooperation begins where competition leaves off" but, rightly understood, good competition is a helpful form of cooperation.

A focus on *competitive play* and the way it relates to worship will complement the previous chapter's consideration of *intellectual, physical* and *imaginative* forms of play. There are two aspects of competitive play that have useful parallels with worship: firstly, the value of having a contest

---

7. Huizinga, *Homo Ludens*, 31.

8. Andy Murray, *The Age* (Melbourne), January 17, 2013.

and, secondly, the implications of the unpredictability of outcome that is part of every contest.

Competition is a central concept in play although it occurs in various degrees. In ice hockey the agonistic element—the contest between players—often seems excessively fierce, extending beyond competitiveness in scoring goals into brutal physical attacks on opponents. Croquet, on the other hand, appears much more genteel—at least until one gets involved in a serious competition, when, I am assured, it can become quite heated! In various ways competitiveness is essential in everything from poker to pickup sticks, from conkers to canasta and from tennis to twenty questions. Competition—the real testing of one's ability—is what makes many games enjoyable. A contest between teams adds a new dimension to kicking a football around; it gives a greater purpose than simply developing one's individual skill.

Competition also makes the game relational. Frequently one is working *with* a team of people as well as competing *against* others though, as parents and coaches frequently point out, having an opponent does not necessarily mean having an enemy. Though one might play "against" an opponent most people can recognize that they are essential for the game and that there is a real sense in which they are playing "with" them as much as with their own team. In having an opponent one can enjoy the game, respect what they do, applaud their skill and be friends with them. Yet through all this the competitive attitude remains important.

Associated with this competitiveness, and equally important, is the unpredictability of the contest. In a real contest one cannot predict how the game will develop, what the final outcome will be or who, if anyone, will be the winner. In most games and sports if one knew the result at the beginning there would be little point in playing at all. In this case an absence of knowledge is a good and essential thing.

So, competition and unpredictability are essential, positive and healthy aspects of many games but, much more significantly than this, they are central to life as a whole. Huizinga argues that the agonistic dimension of play is central in understanding nothing less than the emergence of civilization. His bold claim is that every significant achievement that takes human society forward is the result of playful competition and contest. "Culture" he says, "arises in the form of play." The desire to do better than others have done is the driving force in science, law, philosophy, business, art, warfare, poetry and music.

After examining the evidence in each area he concludes that "civilization is *played* . . . it arises *in* and *as* played, and never leaves it."[9]

Research and innovation in every area takes place through having an imaginative, creative and, especially, competitive attitude. This drives people to "play around" with the objective natural world, and subjective abstract ideas, in order to do better and better, and from this new technological, aesthetic and cultural possibilities emerge. Work and the attitudes associated with it are very important to a society but will rarely bring about the new possibilities that play does. A culture that takes itself and its life too seriously and insufficiently playfully will decline rather than advance. It is in those times, places, attitudes and movements where competitive playfulness is valued that society moves forward.

Competition and unpredictability are equally important in worship. It would certainly be wrong to suggest that planning and order are not helpful or that God is not experienced in liturgical repetition or routine. God frequently speaks through the familiar and the habitual. In his first letter to the Corinthians the apostle dealt with the issue of some very disorderly worship where people were interrupting one another. Some were actively vying with each other to be able to prophesy, others were bringing unintelligible messages, while others were chattering and interrupting. In response Paul insisted on the appropriateness of control and order, "for God is not a God of disorder . . . everything should be done in a fitting and orderly way" (1 Cor 14:33–40). It always remains a matter for judgment. That is, a concern for planning and order ought to be matched with a sensitivity to the fact that God's actions are not always predictable. Unfortunately, as a new pastor I inadvertently spent some years trying to ensure that there was *no* unpredictability in the worship services that I led. This did not mean keeping the form of worship exactly the same each week because I was leading worship in an ecumenical congregation of three denominations where we sought to explore a variety of liturgical forms. In that congregation the use of the imagination and creativity in worship was highly valued, my planning was detailed and we constantly changed the liturgical form. But those of us leading the worship, especially me, sought to plan so thoroughly that we would always know exactly what was going to happen in every respect. We aimed at establishing in advance the spiritual outcome that the congregation would have, whether a renewal in some aspect of faith, repentance, praise, thanksgiving or commitment to a particular concept or idea. This was good and

9. Huizinga, *Homo Ludens*, 46 and 173.

helpful and the worship was often appreciated, except that in establishing outcomes and removing unpredictability it tended to control the movement of the Spirit. Who can predict what God will *really* want to do? Excessive control can ultimately be unhelpful and restrictive.

Eventually, as time went by, the problem was recognized and responding to it meant learning to read the way the worship was going. It involved planning just as thoroughly, but it also meant being aware of the Spirit and of the corporate experience of the congregation, and then during the worship, if it was helpful, being equally willing to stay with, let go of, or perhaps modify the plans that had been made. It never meant preparing any less but it did mean listening more. The unpredictability that was important was the unpredictability of God.

Competing with God

It is one thing to argue that there is an unpredictable dimension in worship just as there is in play, but does worship involve any form of contest or competition? Are we playing against anyone in worship? The short, and perhaps disconcerting, answer is that we are playing against God.

It seems rather strange to think about playing against God and it is reasonable to ask whether the play analogy is breaking down at this point. Is it appropriate to play against God? Indeed, does it make any real sense to think of playing against someone who knows everything and can do anything? A somewhat less but still rather one-sided contest occurred some years ago when the organizers allowed a computer chess program called Fritz to take part in the Dutch national chess championships. The results of matches against Fritz counted towards determining the champion, and although Fritz would not receive the prize money that was on offer it was eligible to win the championship. Some people boycotted the event, one competitor who refused to play against Fritz was deemed to have lost, and others complained. Chess programs may be fun and challenging but the question was whether it was a mismatch to allow a program that could recall a huge database of previous plays and analyze millions of possibilities to compete against people in a national championship. Initially it might seem that playing against God is even more of a mismatch, but actually it is quite different because, even though God's knowledge and power are greater than that of a computer, God relates—and competes—with people in a personal and interactive manner, rather than purely mechanically. A contest with a personal God is quite possible.

Genesis 32 describes one very unusual contest with God where Jacob wrestled at night with a mysterious stranger. This was not a fight between enemies but had more of the atmosphere of a contest of strength, albeit a tense one, between friends—the kind of wrestling that boys and young men typically enjoy engaging in with their friends. In the midst of it there was a cryptic conversation that illuminates the meaning of the wrestling. At daybreak the man asked Jacob to let him go, but Jacob said, "I will not let you go unless you bless me." In response, the man indicated that Jacob would no longer be known as Jacob but as Israel (meaning "he struggles with God"), because he had struggled with God and had overcome. Jacob then asked to know the man's identity but instead received the blessing he sought. He then declared that the place would now be called Peniel, "because I saw God face to face, and yet my life was spared." Jacob engaged in a contest not merely with a man but with God and, even more significantly, the man told him, "you have overcome."

Abraham also engaged in a contest with God, although of a more verbal kind, about whether the righteous people in Sodom ought to be swept away along with the unrighteous. Abraham feared that God's judgment would lead to this (although the account in Genesis 18 does not say that this is what God was necessarily going to do) and he seemed to win the concession that if there were fifty righteous people then the city would be saved. Then Abraham argued that forty-five should be enough, and gained God's promise that the city would not be destroyed. He then tried forty and then thirty and twenty and, incredibly, gained a further promise from God not to destroy the city if ten righteous people were found. Abraham too was able to contest matters with God.

As noted previously, in many games our opponent is not, in fact, our enemy but one who is actually working with us and helping us. I play competition tennis each week and so I play each week with the same team and against a different opposition. Obviously, my team tries to work together and aims at helping each other play in the best way possible against the opposition but, in truth, although we are doing our best to beat them we are playing with them much more than we are playing against them. In achieving our goal of enjoying the game, appreciating the exercise, developing our skills and engaging with others the opposition are as important as one's own team. Indeed, it is the opposition who really do the job of encouraging one to be a better player because they allow for a more sustained testing, they reveal more about the faults and areas of need in one's play and they often demonstrate a better way to go about it. Without them there is no game, no testing of skill, no fun or enjoyment and, in the end, no friendship. At the end of the match we sit down together and enjoy one another's company. We want good opposition, because without them there simply is no game. In the right atmosphere even losing can mean winning!

In prayer and worship it is possible to engage in a contest with God in which we compete in order to challenge ourselves to do the very best, to be the very best person that we can be. One part of this contest may be like Jacob's wrestling, though there are numerous forms of this. Firstly, it can be wrestling to believe the promises of God. That is, in the face of life's experiences of tragedy, disappointment, abuse and loss it can be difficult to believe that the kingdom is both present and coming in fullness; it can be hard to trust in the grace of God and difficult to demonstrate hope in the resurrection. Faith means wrestling to secure these things. Secondly, there can be a wrestling to change our nature to overcome the effects of sin and to live in the way to which Christ calls us. This is the struggle between God's Spirit and our human nature. And thirdly, there can be a wrestling with God's call on our lives, to overcome the resistance we feel to a leading that we believe to be from God. In these and other ways we engage in a competition with God. Most of the time, if we are fortunate, we will lose.

There are, however, perhaps even better analogies of the kind of competition that we can engage in with God, as when we play a game with one we love rather than just with some other person who happens to be our opponent for the day. Indeed, play with those one loves the most makes for the best kind of game.

Hafiz, or Shams-ud-din Muhammad (c. 1320–1389), was a Persian poet who wrote about God as his Friend, the Beloved, the Beautiful One. He said, "I am a hole in a flute that the Christ's breath moves through—listen to this music." One of his poems about playing chess with God has been rendered into English by Daniel Ladinsky in this way:[10]

Tripping Over Joy

What is the difference
Between your experience of Existence
And that of a saint?

10. Ladinsky, *I Heard God Laughing*, 66.

The saint knows
That the spiritual path
Is a sublime chess game with God

And that the Beloved
Has just made such a Fantastic Move

That the saint is now continually
Tripping over Joy
And bursting out in Laughter
And saying, "I Surrender!"

Whereas, my dear,
I am afraid you still think
You have a thousand serious moves.

Playing, and competing, with God, as with anyone who is truly loved, is
a great joy and a pleasure. One takes pleasure is seeing the Beloved make
such a fantastic move even though it is against you. It produces amazement
and laughter. In the face of such brilliance what can one do but happily con-
cede, "I surrender!" We should, of course, laugh at the idea that our moves
might be better than the Beloved's. It is, of course, possible to play with the
Beloved with the attitude that one wants to do nothing other than win. In
which case, in the face of a brilliant move, one might refuse to surrender
and delude oneself into thinking that playing other moves might bring a
victory. In this case one is continuing with the game while having lost the
sense of play. It is much better to play to love rather than to win. In which
case one wins even when one loses.

Playing with the Idea of Play

Playing in Relationships

This chapter discusses playing with others as well as with God. Many people today say that they want spirituality without religion, often meaning, "I want my own form of spirituality without having to worry about what others say or do." But just as most playing is best done with other people so too is spiritual development. Reflect on the way you play, in an ordinary sense and in spiritual ways, with other people. Are you able to identify any connections, parallels or discontinuities? This chapter also discusses both competing and cooperating (both are essential) in playing games. Do you see this in your own play with God and others?

5

Theology: Ludic(rous) Thinking

Do but observe our grim philosophers
that are perpetually beating their brains on knotty subjects,
and for the most part you'll find them grown old
before they are scarcely young!

—DESIDERIUS ERASMUS

The theologian who has no joy in
his work is not a theologian at all.

—KARL BARTH

In his satirical attack on the superstitious piety of his day, *In Praise of Folly*, Desiderius Erasmus (1469–1536), the most renowned scholar of his age, rightly poked fun at those who could not engage in theological reflection joyfully. "Do but observe our grim philosophers" he noted, "that are perpetually beating their brains on knotty subjects, and for the most part you'll find them grown old before they are scarcely young!"[1] And although Karl Barth is renowned for long and detailed theological reflections he believed that "(t)he theologian who has no joy in his work is not a theologian at all."[2] Too often the joy and playfulness of eternal life has been lost in the midst of theological discussions that are important, detailed and thought-provoking but nonetheless earnest and humorless.

1. Erasmus, *Praise of Folly*, 25.
2. Barth, *Church Dogmatics*, II.1:656.

59

It is not only theologians that ought to express joy; every church ought to exhibit a playful or *ludic* nature. But it would be a mistake to think that this important characteristic is found in social, sporting or recreational groups in the church. Such forms of play are socially and culturally important but are often peripheral to the life of the body of Christ. A congregation's true ludic nature is not primarily seen in a proliferation of happy social activities but in *joyful, creative, imaginative, adventurous worship and mission*. It is not enough to add on some fun activities and think that this is healthy if, at the same time, the essential dimensions of church life resist all playful attitudes.

Unfortunately, there is an ongoing, though often unexpressed, difference of opinion within the church between those who are very happy to express a playful attitude in the church's spiritual life and those who are less keen on it. Occasionally people have taken an explicitly negative view of play, seeing it in the light of various biblical warnings ("Woe to you who laugh . . ." and "Nor should there be obscenity, foolish talk or coarse joking . . .; Luke 6:25; Eph 5:4) as being spiritually dangerous. A long time ago Ambrose warned his clergy against joking and, similarly, Augustine warned against the pleasures of the table, of playing and joking. Even today, when it is less likely that there will be such explicit directives, and even though there may be special occasions of celebration, it is common for churches to have a default position of a certain due reverence. This reflects the view that while play is suitable for other contexts, and occasionally appropriate in worship, it is not the usual approach as it conflicts with the notion of reverential worship, humble prayer and sacrificial ministry.

The Forgotten Virtue

Consequently, the notion of a playful attitude as a distinct theological virtue is, for some, a step too far. But not for Hugo Rahner, who wrote most notably on this topic and rightly described eutrapelia as "the forgotten virtue" in his book *Man at Play*. It is certainly a neglected theme. Indeed, how many could list the seven cardinal "heavenly virtues" let alone a relatively minor virtue like eutrapelia? Most people would probably have a better chance of listing the "seven deadly *sins*" (lust, gluttony, greed, sloth, wrath, envy and pride) than they would of naming the corresponding "seven heavenly *virtues*." The traditional seven are a combination of the four cardinal virtues derived from Greek philosophy (wisdom, courage, temperance and justice) and three theological virtues (faith, hope and love). Reformed theology, however, has always argued that one's understanding of the moral life cannot be predicated on the natural/supernatural distinction involved in this listing and has preferred to derive a catalog of essential virtues from biblical lists such as Galatians 5:22–23 (love, joy, peace, patience, kindness, goodness, gentleness, faithfulness and self-control). But whichever approach one takes, eutrapelia or playfulness does not usually appear unless one looks further down the extended catalog of lesser virtues found in Aristotle and Aquinas.

Eutrapelia, Rahner points out, began its virtuous life as a balanced or average state of being in between taking everything too seriously and never taking anything seriously. As Rahner puts it, "poor Eutrapelia has led a miserable existence in the standard books of moral theology . . . as a virtuous neutral attitude, upholding the mean in recreational play and joking."[3] Rahner, however, seeks to develop its characteristics so that it takes on a more positive, playful character (an attitude consistent with the book's rather quirky and questioning subtitle, "Did You Ever Practice Eutrapelia?"). David Miller says of Rahner,

> Rahner's theology refocuses contemporary scholarship of the Christian religion on what has been so lacking in the overly serious and pedantic tomes of much past theology; it focuses on the true "enjoyment" and the delightful hilarity that is supposed properly to be the end of Christianity's salvific grace.[4]

Despite Rahner's enthusiasm for eutrapelia as a lightness of being that provides a balance between work and play, between seriousness and fun, and between the responsibilities of ministry and the joy of worship, it does, in the end, retain echoes of simply being "a cautious average."

An alternative is the Latin based "ludicity" (which is not, it should be noted despite the perpetual efforts of my spell-checker to change it, the same as lucidity). This comes from "ludus," meaning play, and *Homo Ludens* was used as the title of the classic book on play by Johan Huizinga. But ludicity does not, for most people, communicate as much as the more common terms "fun", "play" and "playfulness." The problem with these more well-known terms, though, is that they seem too trivial or lightweight for what is being described as a philosophically and theologically important mode of being.

---

3. Rahner, *Man at Play*, 91

4. Miller, *Gods and Games*, 86.

And so there is a temptation to forego the simple "fun" for the more theologically heavyweight "joy" and to avoid the potentially lightweight "playful" and use the more serious-sounding "ludicity" or "eutrapelia."

There is a strong biblical and theological argument for including ludicity among the essential characteristics of the Christian life even though the word itself does not appear in biblical lists of virtues. Ludicity should be seen as a general attitude to the whole of life in the same way that a work ethic is more than simply an approach to one's work—it is a way of approaching everything, but in this case, playfully. Play is wide-ranging (children, musicians, athletes, thespians and more all play—it is what people do) in which everything is linked by the sheer pleasure involved in doing it. Playing transcends reality; it allows one to experience any one of a huge range of imaginary worlds with their own rules (or lack of them) but all characterized by freedom, creativity, engagement, joy and fun. This sort of playfulness ought to be part of the Christian ethos, a way of living in the kingdom because it can be seen as a way of being conformed to the image of God (Col 3:10). This is because the image of God that humanity bears is not found in some static imprint but in living as God lives—creatively, joyfully, freely and playfully.

The use of "ludicity" as a description of playfulness would probably please G. K. Chesterton. He expressed disappointment at his own writings when he was only able to be theologically serious, rather than playful or humorous, due to the limitations of a deadline, and so he would appreciate the fact that using "ludicity" and its cognates does at least allow one the happy option of describing it all as "a ludicrous systematic theology!"

Play Theory

A ludicrous theology needs to pay attention to what other disciplines, such as sociology, psychology and anthropology, have learned about play and that means, as is often the case in any formal area of study, beginning with a definition of what one is investigating. In one way this is very simple as everyone knows when they are playing, but when it comes to precise definition, play, like art, can be surprisingly elusive. This has led to a variety of approaches to the topic that will be discussed below. Although it may sound as though it has been structured in accordance with a numerology derived from the book of Revelation or the gospel of John, it is quite unplanned for there to be seven different approaches with the seventh one having seven dimensions. (Incidentally, one may note that not all games are simple; some games require considerably more effort than others but, in return, they can also produce greater benefits. Everyone has their limit in regard to the time and effort they will put into a particular game and it could be that some will consider the effort involved in exploring seven different approaches to play theory to simply be too much. If you are in that category you might like to scan quickly or even skip over the rest of this chapter to move on to the next chapter and a consideration of the relationship between grace, work and play. Those who like to have good theoretical foundations will stay with this chapter and get to that issue a little later.)

Theories of Play

The first approach is to define play by representatively (or perhaps even comprehensively) *listing the games and activities* that are considered to be play.[5] If one was following Johannine numerology there would probably be seven categories here as well but, in reality, there are numerous forms of categorization. Such a listing might well include reference to team games (various sports, cards, board games), mind games (daydreams and fantasy), solitary games (solitaire or patience), pretend games (play-acting, "let's pretend"), casual play (jokes, tricks), celebrations (balls, festivals) and games of risk (hang gliding, bungy jumping) but the problem with this approach is that the categories are endlessly flexible and the creation of a comprehensive list impossible. Even if one achieved a comprehensive list and a useful categorization there is, in the end, no actual definition.

A second approach is to define play by *describing the primary qualities* that are expressed in play. Huizinga lists a number of defining characteristics (although the precise number he nominates can be reckoned in various ways). (1) Play is nothing other than *human freedom*. It is a voluntary activity that no one can be commanded to engage in, because that which is commanded is no longer play (though it may be an imitation of it). This is not to say that children and adults are not, by nature, compelled to play. They feel an instinct to do so but nonetheless engage in it freely. (2) Play creates *its own world* that is outside of the "real" or "ordinary" world. Those playing are, of course, aware that they are "only pretending" or doing it "just

---

5. Note that the English linguistic distinction between "play" and "game" is not found in most other European languages; "play/game" is "jouer/jeu" (French), "spielen/spiel" (German), "jugar/juego" (Spanish), "giocare/gioco" (Italian).

for fun" (though this does not prevent it from proceeding with the utmost seriousness). (3) Play operates as an interlude in daily life, occurring *within its own time and space*. Players know when they are playing; they are aware of its limitations. (4) Play creates a world *with its own order* and, in this way, is connected to the creation of beauty. Play has an aesthetic dimension. (5) Play involves a degree of *tension and uncertainty*. The player is attempting to achieve something, to succeed, and there is always the possibility of losing or failing. But there is great satisfaction with success. (6) Play is only possible because *it has its own rules*. The one who transgresses is a spoilsport or a cheat who threatens the illusion of the play. (7) Play loves to surround itself with *secrecy*. Within the play the laws and customs of ordinary life no longer count, the player is playing a different part, another role, is another being, different from the common world.[6]

Huizinga's list of characteristics has been influential, though he has been critiqued for emphasizing the competitive dimension of play more than others. Another, similarly useful list of characteristics from Pat Power nominates eight qualities of play but stresses pleasure and humor more than tension and competition.[7] Play is (1) *dynamic* ("a feeling of energized freedom" which manifests itself in adults as imagination and creativity); (2) *interactive* (playfulness is always engaging, both internally and externally); (3) *enigmatic* (playfulness inhabits the borderlands of reality and fantasy, of earnestness and frivolity, of sense and nonsense; it involves novelty, paradox, irony and unpredictability); (4) *lighthearted* (it is fun even when the players are very serious); (5) *humorous* (a feeling of lightheartedness, often accompanied by humor and laughter, puns and jokes—the ludic easily becomes ludicrous!); (6) *imaginative* (to feel playfulness is to feel the optimistic energy of imaginative possibility); (7) *open-minded* (there is a freedom from many of the usual cultural, political and personal constraints); and (8) *transformative* (the world of play is transformed from the mundane).

Both attempts to characterize play are helpful in delineating its most important dimensions. Someone exhibiting a number of these characteristics in an activity is almost certainly playing. However, it is uncertain as to which ones, or how many, would *definitively* define play, as one could also be engaged in a number of them and yet be doing something other than playing. This raises the question as to whether there is any way of *defining one central principle* that is both truly essential and completely distinctive

6. Huizinga, *Homo Ludens*, 7–13.

7. Power, "Playing with Ideas," 300.

about play. This is a third approach. It has been suggested, for example, that play is essentially a *free space* in which people simply do whatever they want, and whatever that is is play. Stuart Brown prefers to see *pleasure* as being the heart of play. In *Play: How It Shapes the Brain, Opens the Imagination, and Invigorates the Soul* he describes how pleasure leads to play and, as the book title says, transforms lives.[8] Play, he argues, is the most important factor in being a fulfilled human being. Another possibility is expressed by Huizinga. Although, as noted above, he nominates a list of characteristics as essential, he then focuses on the *competitive* aspect of play as being definitive. He merges what he calls two "basic aspects" of play: that play is both a contest *for* something and a representation *of* something. These functions unite in such a way that the game represents contest (as in archery or chess), or else becomes a contest for the best representation of something (as in dress ups or music). Huizinga examines these dimensions of play through every area of social life and demonstrates their significance. His greatest contribution perhaps lies in demonstrating the way that play is formative in the development of culture as a whole. He primarily demonstrates this by reference to the formation of Western civilization. Play is not to be considered merely as one distinct sphere of life but as an attitude and a set of behaviors essential to every aspect of social life.

Nonetheless, because Huizinga focuses almost exclusively on the role of contest his approach has been challenged (somewhat ironically it must be admitted, as contesting his approach may in fact support the point he is making). Roger Caillois, for example, both follows Huizinga for what he describes as his incredibly fertile approach and yet critiques it because it seeks to provide a single interpretation for so many diverse activities. The mere fact of a single name for them all, he argues, is not sufficient to demonstrate that activities with such different qualities and aspects are truly one.[9] A recognition of these differences is, he argued, important but it is not surprising that different scholars choose to focus on one or the other. Caillois himself sees a degree of integration in the way the various forms of play unite in *the creation of a different world*. He distinguishes four different forms of play: competition (e.g., archery and chess), chance (e.g., gambling), simulation (e.g., fantasy and pretend) and disorder (or vertigo, such as tumbling down a hill or spinning around).[10] Games of competition and chance are opposites

8. Brown, *Play*, 13.
9. Caillois, *Man and the Sacred*, 154.
10. Caillois, *Man, Play and Games*, 12.

(the former seeking control and the latter recognizing the complete absence of it) yet when combined they reflect normal life. The other forms of play also have the effect of creating a simulated world—in fantasy the player takes on another role than the one they usually have, and in disordered play the common mode of perception is suspended and another is experienced. In short, play is all about creating another world.

Its multifaceted nature means that freedom, pleasure, contest and the creation of another world each have their advocates as being the principal characteristic of play. But it is a subject that resists easy categorization and consequently, sometimes clarity has been sought by a fourth approach, *the way of negation*, by which something is defined by what it is *not*. This is exemplified in the attempt to define the *opposite* of play. Work is popularly dichotomized with play but it is more of a correlate with play than an opposite to it, and it is Brian Sutton-Smith's observation that depression is the opposite of play that, in the end, has tended to gather most support. Play is an attitude expressing freedom, delight and creativity while depression is a state that is unable to express any of these. This approach reinforces the point that play is neither a diverse set of activities nor any one particular behavior, but rather *a state of being*.

Related to this, although philosophically distinct, is a fifth approach that is seen in Jacques Derrida's lecture "Structure, Sign and Play in the Discourse of the Human Sciences," delivered in 1966, that is often reckoned to be the beginning of poststructuralism. Derrida denies the dichotomy between subject and object, appearance and reality or, as he describes, between reality and free play. Play is not mimetic or imitative or life; play is simply the way that we live and in *playing with* the ambiguities and inconsistencies of life it points towards the impossibility of a single unified meaning. This view of play as *the form of life* (or life as a form of play) can be related to Huizinga's insights into play as the whole of social life, although Derrida's deconstructionist stress on the ambiguities and tensions of life/play means that it is worked out very differently.

Another way of integrating the various dimensions of play that have emerged is by *reference to their evolutionary origins*. This is our sixth approach to play. Brian Sutton-Smith, a leading theorist on play, for example, hypothesizes regarding a comprehensive theory of play with what he refers to as "adaptive layers" of meaning. The first layer sees play as an evolutionary adaptation that emerges in the midst of threat and danger, with play as a way of emulating and avoiding serious conflict by replacing it with play and ritual. The second adaptive layer looks at the more reflexive and reflective dimension whereby play emerges ahead of time, as an activity that not only replaces conflict but provides exercises that help when real conflict occurs. Adaptive layer number three recognizes the duality of primary and secondary emotions. Some emotions (such as shock, anger, fear, disgust and sadness) lie behind certain types of play, such as contests and risk-taking exercises, but other emotions (such as happiness, pride, empathy, guilt and shame) lie behind the rules and traditions involved in rituals and more expressive forms of play. The fourth layer of development notes that play influences the way one feels about oneself. One can experience courage, humor, success and many other emotions. "This is play being valued in ontological terms. One wins or loses but most importantly one feels differently about oneself, somehow more fulfilled, perhaps more accomplished."[11]

Having considered genetic effect, affective influences, personal performance, the multilayered approach moves on to cultural factors. The next adaptive layer considers the way various cultural scripts determine the perception of play. Contests, for example, tend to take place more often in societies that value hunting and warfare or where criminals and entrepreneurs abound; subjective, experiential play tends to take place in cultures that are individualistic and consumer-orientated and games of chance exist more prominently in societies with strong beliefs in spiritual controls.

Rhetorics of Play

The seventh and final approach is also best illustrated in the work of play theorist Sutton-Smith, who has brought together what he refers to as *seven rhetorics of play*, by which he is referring to the various traditions of interpretation of play that have emerged in different cultures.[12] He divides them into ancient and modern. The modern rhetorics include notions of play as *progress* (play in education, as personal development), *imagination* (play as art, creativity, science and culture) and *selfhood* (play as freedom, the expression of individuality, personal happiness). The first of these rhetorics is commonplace in educational and psychological theory. Play is interpreted in functional terms as a means of learning and developing. The first time play was formally incorporated into modern educational curricula was in the Victorian period, when physical exercise and sport were introduced. It

11. Sutton-Smith, *Ambiguity of Play*, 115.

12. Ibid.

was soon seen as critical for development and is exemplified in the probably misquoted but nonetheless oft-repeated and influential saying attributed to the Duke of Wellington that "The battle of Waterloo was won on the playing fields of Eton." Today play is widely seen as important in learning and essential for healthy personal development. This relates to the first of the ancient rhetorics, that of play as *power* (play as contest in sport, markets, law, war). In play one reflects the conflicts of life and, indeed, trains for them. The gymnasium and the colosseum are illustrative of this.

The second of the ancient rhetorics identifies play with the formation of *identity*. This occurs in a more corporate way than is found in the modern rhetorics of imagination (with its focus on interior mental processes) and selfhood (with the notion that we are truly ourselves when we play, away from the obligations of work) for it takes place in corporate ritual and festival.

The third of the ancient rhetorics sees play as *fate* (involving chance, gambling and risk). In both play and real life people are subject to forces beyond their control in a way the modern mind resists. William Shakespeare's well-known statement "All the world's a stage, and all the men and women merely players" from a speech in *As You Like It* expresses this point of view. A tension between freedom and determinism is found, with varying emphasis on each, in both ancient and modern rhetorics. The ancient rhetoric speaks of fate but many nonetheless believe that struggle and effort will achieve something. The modern rhetoric stresses personal freedom and control but also needs to take into account those events and circumstances that inevitably limit the possibilities. Play is an image of life that can incorporate both dimensions.

The seventh and final rhetoric is both ancient and modern and is the most obvious and most universal interpretation of all: it is the recognition of play as *frivolity* (laughter, foolishness, subversion). This is not only arguably the most characteristic of all the characteristics of play but it is also the one that perhaps creates the greatest initial problem for any correlation or identification of play with the sacred. For many the lightheartedness, the unpredictability and the fantasy of play appears to trivialize the spiritual life. There is a tendency to focus on alternative, more serious dimensions of the religious endeavor, such as service, sacrifice and commitment, and a few see direct conflicts between the lighthearted characteristics of play and the painful problems of life and a theology of the cross.

Obviously, careful theological justification is required for any connection between play and theology but, interestingly, a justification also emerges from within play theory so that the correlation of play and spirituality has an internal justification rather than one imposed from outside. For a number of theorists play is connected with the sacred.

Play and the Sacred

Huizinga's *Homo Ludens: A Study of the Play-Element in Culture* is the result of an extensive review of play across cultures and eras. He examines a wide range of dimensions of play and, in the end, concludes that "civilization cannot exist in the absence of a certain play-element."[13] Play has characteristics that are essential for the formation of human culture, including the ability to imagine and create a new world that has not previously existed. The competitive dimension of play is also critical in the development of every area of art, science and culture. Huizinga's cross-cultural examination is extensive and, in the end, having earlier carefully avoided "the philosophical short circuit that would assert all human action to be play," he finds that this notion cannot be denied. He affirms the teaching of Plato that humanity is made as God's "plaything" and that life must be lived as play and quotes the book of Proverbs that speaks of Wisdom playing with God at the creation of the world. This, however, occurs on the final couple of pages of the book and while it is, in one sense, the climax of his reflections it also resembles the "to be continued" notice that sometimes appears at the end of a novel or a movie.

Roger Caillois is one who continuea this line of investigation and he both follows and critiques Huizinga's work. He observes that the identification of play and the sacred is "the most daring" thesis of Huizinga's book and at the same time "the most precarious." For Caillois the congruency between play and the sacred is inescapable but there can be no complete identification between them. He comments, "I do not believe that the various forms of play and of religion, because they are separated with equal care from daily life, occupy equivalent situations with respect to each other, nor that for this reason they are identical in content."[14] That is, although the *forms* of religion and play are similar the *content* is very different. In play the game is invented by the player, who is fully in control (establishing the

13. Huizinga, *Homo Ludens*, 211–13.
14. Caillois, *Man and the Sacred*, 158.

conditions, the time and the limits of the game) and essentially pleasing him or herself; while in relationship with the sacred the play is created by the other and the human player is completely defenseless, never in control and essentially serving another. Moreover, in terms of the relationship between play and daily life it is play that is relaxation, a distraction from everyday dangers and cares, while in the relationship between the sacred and daily life the situation is reversed: the sacred is dangerous, uncontrollable and difficult while everyday world is relaxing and a distraction. In play one is removed from reality while in religion one comes to true reality. So Caillois suggests that "a sacred-profane-play hierarchy needs to be established to balance Huizinga's analysis. The sacred and play resemble each other to the degree that they are both opposed to the practical life, but they occupy symmetrical situations with regard to it."[15] For Caillois religious liturgy is in the form of a game, but if one considers the contents of sacrifice and communion then "one is fully in the sacred and as far removed from play as is conceivable."[16]

Huizinga was right to avoid an a priori identification of play with life because such a connection could only come after a thorough examination of the cultural evidence; and Caillois is right to avoid a simplistic identification of play with the sacred on the basis of external form because the different content of play and religion needs to be addressed. But in the end the connection is valid. Play does not provide a simple explanation for the sacred, but play, life and the sacred are overlapping concepts that share attributes and mutually inform each other. Caillois, for example, characterizes play as the seeking of pleasure for the self and religion as serving another, yet this apparent dichotomy is not absolute because while in play one might begin with a desire for pleasure for the self, one can soon learn that giving pleasure to one's playmate (while perhaps denying it to oneself) is itself a moral good to be repeated.

Psychologists examine the contribution play makes to the healthy development of children; therapists utilize play to uncover attitudes and teach new ways of dealing with problems; sociologists understand play in terms of its function within the community (such as in group building and expressing social order); anthropologists consider its cultural role (in conflict and sexuality, for instance); philosophers consider its connection with meaning in life and theologians reflect on the role of play in

15. Ibid., 160.
16. Ibid., 161.

relationship to God and the world. It should be noted, however, that this is more of a playful theology than a theology of play. It would be possible to undertake a theological examination of the techniques, purposes and effects of the play of children and adults but there is here less interest in play as an activity in itself than in the way that play and a playful attitude influence our understanding of relationship with God, the church and the world. This playful theology considers traditional theological themes and spiritual concepts in the light of a playful attitude. This, then, is a study of the way that playfulness is significant as a model of, or metaphor for, a person's self-perception, their relationship with God and others and the form and meaning of the relationships found within the church. And although Caillois's reservations about an overidentification of play and the sacred is echoed by some theologians, such as Jürgen Moltmann, it will be argued here that even the most difficult concepts of sacrifice, death and the cross can be illuminated by reference to play. As M. A. Screech put it, there can be "laughter at the foot of the cross."[17]

Playing with the Idea of Play

Playing with Concepts and People

Theology involves both "thinking" about the nature of God and faith and also "living this out" in practice. So there are two short games you could play. Firstly, take one of the following concepts and try and discuss it in terms of play and a play attitude: ministry, church, salvation, baptism, evangelism, resurrection. Secondly, for fun, and to explore the idea further with someone else, ask someone if they ever practice eutrapelia and then discuss the ideas that emerge.

---

17. Screech, *Laughter at the Foot of the Cross.*

6

Grace: Creating a Play Ethic

What, then, is the right way of living?
Life must be lived as play.

—PLATO[1]

Real civilization cannot exist in the
absence of a certain play-element.

—JOHAN HUIZINGA[2]

It is somewhat ironic that the church of the Reformation, which stressed the free grace of God in fierce opposition to justification by works, then produced a form of the Christian life in which the only serious activity was work! While the future kingdom of God could be characterized in terms of joy, dance, song and play, the present Christian life came to be dominated by the twin notions of one's *daily work* as a service in the secular realm to God and community and one's *ministry* as a form of spiritual work exhibiting service, commitment, responsibility and sacrifice. The result of this paradoxical transformation of the gospel of grace into the Protestant work ethic was, one might say, somewhat tongue-in-cheek but without exaggeration, that many Christians follow the Dr. Seuss theory of life, as expressed in *The Cat in the Hat Comes Back!*: "This was no time for play. This was no

---

1. Plato, *Laws*, 803–4.
2. Huizinga, *Homo Ludens*, 211.

time for fun. This was no time for games. There was work to be done!"[3] Unfortunately, the very positive elements of the work ethic were distorted by the elimination of those elements of life that are intrinsic to play—a playful attitude, joy, creativity, freedom and doing something with apparently no external product or benefit at all. According to the most common understanding of the Protestant work ethic, the only possible benefit of these activities was that they enabled a person to recuperate in order to return to those work-related activities that are more appropriate for servants of the King and of benefit to the kingdom of God.

Consequently, it is important for Christians, and the church as a whole, to develop a more sustainable *play ethic* that can complement the positive elements of the more dominant work ethic. A play ethic is not opposed to a work ethic, only to distorted forms of it, and to misconceived ideas of the nature of work. Indeed, embracing play as a valuable part of the daily spiritual life of the believer means restoring to work that element of its character, which is often lost or ignored. Work and play need reintegration because they have, with tragic consequences, been separated for too long. Play conceived of by itself, apart from work, can be self-centered and addictive while work without play does a lot more damage than making Jack a dull boy.

The great Reformer Martin Luther zealously promoted the idea that salvation comes by grace through faith and, very specifically, not by any human work. In opposing the clerical religiosity of the church of his day his primary aim was to repudiate the idea that either *good works* (of mercy, charity and so forth) or *religious works* (of fasting, worship or religious obedience) could bring salvation, but this inevitably meant, by association, that *secular work* (one's ordinary, daily work) was of no soteriological value either. However, although none of these works could themselves *bring about* justification they were seen as *an effect* of it. They were the fruit of salvation. This is seen in the way that the classic Reformation text of Ephesians 2:8–9, "For it is by grace you have been saved, through faith . . . not by works," is immediately followed in verse 10 the statement that "we are God's handiwork, created in Christ Jesus to do good works, which God prepared in advance for us to do." Consequently, as a corollary to his repudiation of work as the basis of salvation, Luther stressed the importance of work as one of the effects of salvation. And this work not only included specifically religious work but also ordinary, daily work. Thus, for Luther,

3. Seuss, *Cat in the Hat Comes Back!*, 3.

having a vocation or a calling was not something restricted to clergy and the religious orders; everyone's daily work—of any kind—was their vocation. This was a radical change in thinking.

Previously there had been an unfortunate theological distaste for work, which was seen, spiritually, as second-rate. Although this way of thinking was by no means universal, by the time of the late Middle Ages there was form of spiritual elitism that tended towards somewhat dismissive attitudes to the spiritual value of ordinary, especially manual work. There were, of course, significant exceptions to this. Augustine had stressed the value of ordinary work and Thomas Aquinas had described the fact that one's work is a matter of divine providence and thus is a genuine good, although this was qualified by the claim that the monastic life is best of all.[4] Similarly, despite the same kind of qualification about the ascetic or monastic life, John Chrysostom had said, "In worldly matters no man lives for himself, but artisan, and soldier, and husbandman and merchant, all of them contribute to the common good, and to their neighbors advantage."[5] Benedictine monasticism, with its stress on *ora et labora* ("pray and work"), attributed great value to work (so much so that their vast monastic network of various enterprises has led to them being described as "the first capitalists") although, even in that context, the primary work was always the "work of God" (*Opus Dei*)—saying the Divine Office. Altogether, for a thousand years or so, even when ordinary, daily work was affirmed highly and commended as obedience to God, specifically religious works and practices, as distinct from ordinary work were considered to be spiritually superior. Only those who renounced the ordinary world of everyday life in order to take up a religious life of prayer and worship could be considered to be among the "perfect."

There can be no doubt that Luther raised the perceived value of ordinary, daily work. According to Luther it was God who called everyone and placed them in a life situation according to his will and in this way he attributed far greater value to ordinary work, which was now to be seen as nothing less than a task undertaken in response to a divine call equivalent (well, almost equivalent) to a call to eldership or priesthood. Consequently, Luther reasoned, each one should remain in the position which they were in, as the apostle Paul had taught, saying, "each person should live as a believer in whatever situation the Lord has assigned to them, just as God

4. Aquinas, *Summa Theologica*, III, q. 41, art. 2.

5. Chrysostom, *Homilies*, 469.

has called them" (1 Cor 7:17, also see 24). This latter aspect of Luther's approach to work—that there is a distinct spiritual value in maintaining a high level of stability in work, calling and one's social status—is not a part of the work ethic that is so widely adopted today as the result of a greater appreciation of several other strongly Lutheran themes, such as the importance of individual conscience and personal liberty. These promote the notion of the freedom of the individual to move to another position, a better job or a different career. Social mobility is highly valued today and so Paul's apparent injunction to vocational immobility is frequently tested and probably does not really promote the kind of stability that suited the hierarchical medieval social conditions that existed in the sixteenth century. In any event, Paul's examples of the alleged principle of stability are not really parallel to contemporary work and social situations today and Paul appears to be flexible upon its implementation, allowing those bound to a master or a difficult marital situation flexibility in deciding whether to stay or go, with the underlying motive not being about limiting the social status of the individual but about seeking the common good.[6] Luther, however, saw in Paul's teaching a call for stability and, while this may not be appreciated so much today, at the time it did enhance the perceived value of work because it had the effect of stressing the point that even the most humble forms of work are a calling from God that ought not be resisted. It thus gave considerable comfort to those engaged in various forms of lowly work.

Developing a Healthy Work Ethic

Although it was Luther who began the process of sanctifying work the notion of a Protestant work ethic is particularly associated with John Calvin (1509–1564). He taught that men and women live to bring glory to God through their daily work as much as through their worship. Everyone is called to their work by God. "Each individual has his own kind of living assigned to him by the Lord ... so that he may not heedlessly wander about throughout life."[7] Consequently, the human traits of ambition and concern

6. Paul indicates that it is appropriate for a slave to gain their freedom if they can (1 Cor 7:21) although using their condition as a slave might be of greater use; and it is appropriate for those who are single to marry if they must, even though it might ultimately cause distress as the result of persecution (7:28). The underlying motive is not about limiting the individual but seeking the common good, maintaining peace and stability in society as a whole (7:35).

7. Calvin, *Institutes*, III.X.6.

for social status are inappropriate—everyone should be satisfied with doing the work, and being in the situation, that God has provided. But there is no distinction between spiritual and temporal, sacred and secular work and thus all work, no matter how mundane, is important in the sight of God. As George Herbert later expressed it,

> Teach me, my God and king,
> In all things thee to see;
> And what I do in anything
> To do it as for thee.
>
> If done to obey Thy laws,
> E'en servile labors shine;
> Hallowed is toil, if this the cause,
> The meanest work divine.

All work was now considered to be spiritually valuable, seen as a form of worship not only because work glorifies God but also because it serves the common good and thus is thus a fulfilment of the Great Commandment of loving God and neighbor. Being a servant of God therefore meant working hard, being industrious and diligent and demonstrating commitment and responsibility in one's life. The visible evidence of this commitment to God was, naturally, assumed to be success in work.

The logical corollary of this was that a failure to work (through laziness or indulgence) or failure in work (that is, a lack of success in business) became a sign that one was not only not glorifying God but also that perhaps one was not among the elect. Even more worryingly was that a failure to succeed at work because of unfortunate circumstances or a lowly social status could also be interpreted as a negative judgment upon the individual's relationship with God. And so it was not only the deliberately lazy and indulgent who were at risk of criticism but also the unavoidably poor. Thus the very positive attribution of spiritual value to all forms of work had a potentially negative dimension to it. Attributing significant spiritual value to success in business inevitably encouraged the active pursuit of profit and economic growth and implied that a lack of success and the presence of poverty were potential signs of faithlessness.

This was a radical departure from the Christian beliefs of the Middle Ages, where poverty was largely seen as an indication of commitment and service. Those who were poor were the blessed of God and those who took on poverty voluntarily were the most religious. But now poverty was no longer a holy state and even voluntary poverty became problematic. It could be interpreted as an inappropriate attempt to gain salvation by religious "works." And involuntary poverty was no longer a blessed state but a situation that could be seen either as a result of the general sinfulness of the world (in which case there was a responsibility to care for the poor through giving charity and seeking justice) or, even despite apparently unavoidable circumstances, as a sign of a lack of divine blessing as a result of the sin of the poor themselves (in which case they were receiving an appropriate recompense for their sin). Calvin, however, cannot be criticized for this form of misunderstanding that subsequently emerged; it comes about as the result of a lack of breadth in considering the teaching of Scripture.

For Luther, God gives one a vocation and the implication of this is that it is important to remain where one is and undertake it without complaint. Calvin agreed that God gives everyone a vocation but felt that the implication of this is that it is important to move if necessary to ensure that one is in the right place. Luther's approach affirmed the social value of all vocations, including that of being the lowliest serf, and stressed stability—one ought to simply accept one's position in life as given by God and stay where one is. This suited a traditional agricultural context where it was inevitable and customary for people to undertake the same work as their family. On the other hand, Calvin's approach affirmed the individual value of one's vocation, whatever that may be, and stressed the importance of searching it out. This approach suited a more changeable urban context where people undertook businesses that needed to grow and adapt and this therefore encouraged change and movement. Thus, both Luther and Calvin drew culturally helpful but different pastoral implications from the same fundamental fact concerning the divine ordering of human vocation.[8]

---

8. Guidance for lay people in determining their vocation can be deduced from four fundamental principles Calvin used in advising those discerning a call to eldership. First, it must be recognized that a call is something given by God and not primarily a human choice. Yet, secondly, human agency is required to discern it and this involves both the individual concerned and others. The one who is genuinely called ought to be able discern the inner call of God while others should be able to discern the outward effect of such a call on the church. Thirdly, the validity of a call depends on evidence of the necessary gifts and, finally, whether the appropriate personal qualities were displayed. Calvin, *Institutes*, IV, ch. 3, sections 7–12.

Work without Play

The good things of this life—both the material goods that God has given for us to use and the pleasurable activities in which we may participate—are, according to Calvin, to be enjoyed as gifts of God.[9] There is, he argued, to be a balance between over-strictness in limiting them and too great a laxity in the enjoyment of them. He was critical of both those who had been too severe in limiting physical goods and activities to sheer necessity and those who had been too intemperate, which leads to licentious indulgence. The aim, in all things, is to aspire to eternal life. In practice, however, the fundamental message was of frugal living, of the nobility of work and industry and caution regarding the enjoyment of material things and physical activities, such as play. Firstly, the emphasis fell upon work as a spiritual good and play as merely a necessary relief from it. Work is important, and play is only sometimes necessary, and so the more profitable activity of work is always preferable. As the noted Puritan Richard Baxter (1615–1691) said, "It is for action that God maintaineth us and our activities; work is the moral as well as the natural end of power . . . it is action that God is most served and honoured by . . . The public welfare or the good of the many is to be valued above our own."[10] And as the hymn writer Isaac Watts (1674–1748) advised children, one ought to be aware of the little busy bee:

> In works of labour, or of skill,
> I would be busy too;
> For Satan finds some mischief still
> For idle hands to do.[11]

The balance thus leaned markedly in favor of work rather than play because work was seen a calling and as having spiritual significance. A second problem was that it was influenced by the general attitude that the universality of sin and total depravity precludes the Christian from enjoying life too much. The Puritans—some of the more extreme among early English Protestants and, later, an important part of the settlement of North Americ—are particularly associated with this attitude and more generally with the notion of a work ethic. Indeed, the term "Puritan work ethic" is interchangeable with "Protestant work ethic." But it would be wrong to characterize Puritans—let

---

9. Calvin, *Institutes*, III, 10, 1.

10. Baxter, *Christian Directory*, 375–76.

11. Watts, *Poems*, 348.

alone other Protestants of that period—as completely dour and cheerless. They did have fun and believed that God had given many blessings that were to be enjoyed. Children could, for example, play games and sing songs and there were festivals and music and dancing. Yet in both theology and in practice there was a certain seriousness; children's play really required their parent's permission, music was not permitted in church, they were ambivalent about festivals such as Christmas and although there was good reason for banning dramatic performances (because of licentiousness) and games of chance these limitations appear to have had an influence on general attitudes to life. Various forms of playing—not only plays—were associated with sinfulness not least because the children of Israel who did not come into the Promised Land were struck down by God, who "was not pleased with them" because they were sexually immoral, self-indulgent, whinging idolaters who "sat down to eat and drink, and rose up to play" (1 Cor 10:7, Authorized Version). "Play" was seen as the appropriate translation for a word referring to either idolatry or, more likely, sexual immorality. Consequently, "play" developed a number of unfortunate associations.

One problem was that it was associated with what was seen as an inappropriate level of human freedom. Play is necessarily open-ended and subject to chance, the whims of participants and the results of various explorations that take place as the game progresses. Play generally has a high level of freedom and, for some, this seems to run counter to a theology in which everything is predestined. The intrinsic freedom of play therefore seemed inappropriate as a model of life with God. One might think, therefore, that a different understanding of God's action in the world, one that refuted the predestination of all things and stressed the freedom of divine grace, would grant a greater place to play. That would be theologically appropriate but in practice it does not always happen, given that there are many other, even more powerful, influences on the perception of the relationship of work and play. John Wesley (1703–1791), for example, held a high value for work and success in business. His view was that it is the responsibility of the Christian to work and thus to gain as much as one can. There are, of course, limitations: this is to be done according to sensible principles of business (such as not paying too much for goods), ensuring that there is no injury to one's health and eating and sleeping properly. One must also avoid breaking any of God's law—not defrauding or stealing—and not hurt one's neighbor in body or soul. But then, these cautions and restrictions being observed, it is the bounden duty of all who are engaged in worldly business to observe that first and great rule of Christian wisdom with respect to money: gain all you can.

> Gain all you can by honest industry. Use all possible diligence in your calling. Lose no time. If you understand yourself and your relation to God and man, you know you have none to spare. If you understand your particular calling as you ought, you will have no time that hangs upon your hands. Every business will afford some employment sufficient for every day and every hour. That wherein you are placed, if you follow it in earnest, will leave you no leisure for silly, unprofitable diversions. You have always something better to do, something that will profit you, more or less. And "whatsoever thy hand findeth to do, do it with thy might." Do it as soon as possible: No delay! No putting off from day to day, or from hour to hour! Never leave anything till to-morrow, which you can do today. And do it as well as possible. Do not sleep or yawn over it: Put your whole strength to the work. Spare no pains. Let nothing be done by halves, or in a slight and careless manner. Let nothing in your business be left undone if it can be done by labour or patience.[12]

It is well known that this exhortation to *gain* money through hard work was not designed to lead to self-indulgence or the accumulation of wealth. For Wesley it was essential that this first rule be accompanied by two others: that one ought to *save* as much as possible—rather than spend it on oneself or one's family—in order to *give* away all one possibly can. This last rule was, of course, the one that was most likely to be broken or ignored but for Wesley giving as much as one possibly can was critical, not only for the benefit of the poor but for one's own sanctification. Not only was hard, honest work a part of one's calling; giving to the maximum was essential for the development of one's holiness.

Work, for Wesley, was a calling of great personal spiritual value as well as a public good. Play, on the other hand, was a liability and a danger. The cause of Wesley's well-known distaste for play is much debated. It is likely that it emerged as much from his own childhood experiences as from his theological presuppositions. He was home schooled by his mother, Susanna, and school hours were strictly controlled with no time given to play. Play was permitted at other times but only with the family and not with the local village children. After the fire that destroyed their home the Wesley children were temporarily billeted with other families and when

12. Wesley, *Works*, Sermon 50.

they returned home Susanna discovered that they had learned songs as well as some rude and clownish behavior, which she put an end to by requiring Scripture reading instead, and "in the process playing ceased to be part of John's childhood."[13]

Later in his journal Wesley recounted his reading of Jean-Jacques Rousseau's *Émile* concerning education and children. Rousseau (1712–1778) and John Locke (1632–1734) provided the first modern theories of play. They were expressing the views of the Age of Enlightenment with its stress on the intrinsic goodness of human nature, individualism, autonomy and reason.[14] Childhood, seen as being unaffected by original sin and with individual natures ready to be formed, could express these essential ideals in free play and through them grow to independent maturity. Locke and Rousseau differed regarding the relative importance of nature and nurture, with Locke expecting a more guided form of independence for children leading to the development of self-controlled and hard-working gentlemen seeking the good of the whole of society. Rousseau wanted children to have as little guidance as possible to allow the children's own inclinations to lead them to whatever future was appropriate for them. Both saw play as an important part of the developmental process. The contrast between this modern view of childhood and more traditional views could not be sharper. To say that Wesley was disappointed is an understatement. He declared about Rousseau that "a more consummate coxcomb [a foolish, vain and conceited person] never saw the sun! How amazingly full of himself!" Rousseau, he argued, simply did not understand children; his claim that "young children never love old people" was nonsense and his work overall was "grounded neither upon reason nor experience" and was typical of those who "are too wise to believe their Bibles." Yet beyond all that, "I object to his temper, more than to his judgment: he is a mere misanthrope; a cynic all over."[15]

Whether it was his childhood or his theology that was the primary influence, it is the case that at the Kingswood School founded by Wesley playing was not allowed on the basis that playing as a child only resulted in playing as an adult.[16] Wesley's attitude to play is probably a mixture of social and theological factors. On the one hand, he did not have a great comprehension of the needs and the nature of childhood, probably as the

13. Benzie, "As a Little Child," 31.

14. Locke, *Some Thoughts Concerning Education*; and Rousseau, *Émile*.

15. Wesley, *Journal*, February 3, 1770.

16. Wesley, "Short Account of the School in Kingswood," 98.

result of his own upbringing, but on the other hand his focus on childhood was exactly the same as his focus on every other dimension of life—that it is an arena for the development of holiness. Everything was subject to this overarching aim in life and while work provided an opportunity for the development of personal holiness at the same time as achieving a social good, play did not—in his way of thinking—provide the same opportunities and so was seen as being of lesser value.

Play and Moral Development

It would be quite shocking if playing baseball, marbles, jackstones or engaging in any kind of play in the street was illegal—even when the games are condoned and watched over by caring parents. And it would be horrendous if the police in New York City were actively arresting children who played games and if for the past three years no less than twelve thousand children had been arrested each year and taken to court! And it would be even worse if, as a result of this, children were learning to form gangs, set lookouts and find ways to avoid being caught, and if escaping from the police was becoming a new game in itself. Unfortunately, although this is not happening in New York now, the scenario is not an imaginary one; it is what actually happened in 1910–1913 and is recorded by educationalist Joe L. Frost in his study of the history of play.[17] The criminalization of play in the street encouraged children to perceive themselves as criminals and consequently for many children engaging in other crimes, such as fighting and stealing, seemed relatively normal. Play in the street was banned as the result of extensive poverty, the difficulties of rapid population growth and the absence of facilities, but in this situation where there was, admittedly, obvious social difficulty the banning of public play as a solution certainly says a lot about contemporary attitudes concerning the value of children's play. Fortunately, not everyone saw it that way. On April 19, 1913 four hundred volunteer civic workers went onto the streets of New York with maps and tabulation sheets to count and classify all the play that was taking place at precisely 4 p.m. The subsequent report of the People's Institute, *The City Where Crime Is Play*, provided an analysis of street play and was designed to bring about social change. It was part of a wider, international reform movement that began much earlier in the late eighteenth century, which developed in the nineteenth and culminated in the first part of the

17. Frost, *History of Children's Play*, 84–110.

twentieth century. It involved the spread of a new attitude towards education and play and it arose as a direct result of the Enlightenment approach to human nature, personal development and, as seen in Locke and Rousseau, play as a developmental tool. As a result, in the late eighteenth and early nineteenth centuries countries in Europe and America developed various forms of child care, preschools, infant schools, gymnasia, kindergartens (play gardens for children) and public outdoor playgrounds. There was a particular concern for the poor and a desire to eliminate child exploitation at work and to enhance the physical, psychological and moral welfare of children. Education, health care and moral development went hand in hand in the establishment of various institutions and play was an important part of them all as it was seen as enabling the natural development of children. Indeed, this was a play movement that eventually extended well beyond the needs of the child.

> As far back as 1821 there arose a new interest in play which has increased until today. First came the day of the gymnasiums and the outdoor playground, while a little later the small park came into existence. About the time of World War I the play movement reached what has been called civic art and welfare stage. The outstanding feature of this stage was the recognition of the legitimate desire of the people for drama, music, and dancing, on the one hand, and on the other, the recognition of the exploitation of this normal desire by commercialized amusements. The need and value of play has continued to be recognized until today it is seen as something far more comprehensive than organized recreation or the games of children. This broader conception of play shows that it covers a group of activities as wide as the scope of human life.[18]

Play had developed a place in society. Childhood was for education and personal and moral development and play, especially free play, was central to this process. It expressed the autonomy of the individual, allowed for creativity and personal development and was a caring response to poverty, child work practices and exploitation. It was also fun. Children had, of course, always played as they were able, but now play had a social standing and a role to fulfill. It was a legitimate activity and received support and encouragement.

In the relationship between work and play, work was consistently seen as virtuous and play was consistently perceived as, at the very least,

18. Bennett, "Play and Its Meaning," 165–72.

problematic. This is because work and play are assumed to be entities that are alternates to each other—one either works *or* one plays, and if one does more work then there is less play, and vice versa. Consequently, not only did frivolous play suffer when contrasted with virtuous work, but both work and play suffered by this dichotomy whereby they are defined in opposition to each other. The erroneous assumption in this is that work and play are different sorts of activities occurs whenever one defines work in terms of a list of certain activities, such as plumbing and accountancy, and play as being constituted by certain other activities, such as chess and golf. On this view, an activity can't be both at the same time. But this perception of work and play as fundamentally different pursuits that exclude one another leads to a distortion of both. Work without a dimension of play and creativity is drudgery and boredom while play without work is indulgent and self-serving. Work needs play to see things differently, to generate ideas, to encourage participation and experimentation, imagination and passion. Play needs work to prevent it living entirely for itself, being self-centered, uncontrolled, useless and unproductive. Play is only fully enjoyable when one has been working and vice versa.

Integrating Work, Rest, and Play

The polarized view of work and play that has been so unhelpful in many ways can be overcome when both work and play are understood in terms of their relationship to God. Both work and play are forms of relationship with God. Indeed, they are aspects of the worship of God and if seen independently of this are easily distorted. Unfortunately, even the connection of play and work with worship has itself been problematic. Some years ago Gordon Dahl observed that "Most middle-class Americans tend to worship their work, to work at their play, and to play at their worship."[19] That is, he perceived a tendency to attribute great importance to work (which was an outcome of the work ethic), which then needed to be "balanced" with play, leisure and family (and getting the right "work/life balance" became a prominent theme), while worship was trivialized in the sense that it largely became a subjective experience primarily associated with the play-leisure-family dimension of life, in contrast to one's work experience. This largely middle-class, male-orientated conceptualization never did justice to the

19. Dahl, *Work, Play and Worship*, 11–12.

full complexity of the real situation or people's varied experiences but it does point to the importance of reintegrating work and play.

The creation narrative of Genesis 1:1—2:4 describes the creation of the world in terms of a whole series of classifications and distinctions. The most obvious is the way the narrative is structured around creation on seven days, with the first six cataloging the creation of light and dark, day and night, land and sea, vegetation and living creatures each created "according to its kind" and the creation of humanity as male and female. This is not a scientific taxonomy but rather a scheme of classification that has theological, moral and cultic significance. It stresses, theologically, the fact of creation by God according to nothing else than divine utterance, and the comprehensiveness of this work of creation—nothing that exists lies outside of God's creative and sustaining power. It also implies that one ought to have a certain moral respect for the created order because God specifically created it in that way, and it provides a foundation for determining cultic and social practices, distinguishing clean and unclean, determining that which is edible and providing a rationale for not mixing species in breeding, sowing crops or making clothes (e.g., Lev 11 and 19). These distinctions are theologically important.

One of the primary distinctions is between the six days of creative work and the seventh day of sabbath rest. The seventh day is intimately connected with the first six days. It is special and blessed precisely because God has completed the work of creation. This divine rest tells us several important things about God. First, it says that God is not an eternal fidget who simply has to keep on working without a break. God is not a workaholic. His estimation of the value of work is obviously high but it is not everything. God is able to leave work aside and rest—which is, of course, good advice for everyone. Second, the fact that God rests should not be construed as meaning that God was simply worn out and exhausted from the work on the other six days. The almighty God does not need to rest on that account. The rest of the seventh day is better understood as a *resting in* the world that was made; it is specifically a time for an appreciation of the goodness of the world. It is enjoyment of creation, a participation in that which has been made. In God's world both work and rest have an element of play about them. The work of creation that God does is, by definition, creative! It is described in Proverbs 8:22–31 as a work of delight, a playful time of creativity in which the world comes into being. And it is created for the seventh day—that time of appreciation, enjoyment and blessing.

Creation is born in playfulness and has its purpose in delight and appreciation. This applies particularly to humanity, the high point of creation, which comes into being on the final day of creative activity and is then the focus of the second account of creation in Genesis 2:4–25. Humanity, alone of all creation, is created according to the image of God as a creative being whose purpose lies not primarily in the work of caring for the rest of the created order (Gen 1:28) but in resting in communion with others and with God. As the Lord Jesus said later, "The sabbath was made for people, not people for the sabbath" (Mark 2:27). Just as work has its playful dimension, so too does rest. The sabbath is not primarily defined in terms of passivity or a lack of activity; it is a holy day, one set apart for communion with God where the limitation of work is not, in itself, the purpose of the sabbath but rather a means to enable and encourage worship, communion, fellowship and appreciation of God, others and creation. This is what was so damaged by sin. When the biblical account describes the sin of Adam and Eve it not only fractures the relationship with God but also deforms and damages work and, consequently, rest. Work becomes toil, losing its creative, pleasurable, playful dimension, and rest necessarily becomes much more a retreat from the stress and labor of work (Gen 2:17–19). The playful aspect of both work (as creative, pleasurable and satisfying) and rest (as appreciation, delight and joy) is lost.

The restoration of play to both work and rest is nothing less than part of redemption. These are three concepts that belong together. In considering them as partners, however, I am constantly reminded, or perhaps distracted by being reminded, of the famous advertising jingle that was part of childhood for anyone in Australia, Canada, the UK or New Zealand in the 1960s: "A Mars a day helps you work, rest and play." A Mars bar was, indeed, my favorite snack, however, the notion that a sugar and fat fix (however delicious) helps one rest is somewhat fanciful. So it is better to return to the biblical way of integrating these three concepts! Returning the play dimension to work means once again making work a part of humanity's sharing in the creative life of God (and not merely seeing it as a means of survival) and restoring play to rest means making it a genuine re-creation of the person (and not merely recreation). Work, rest and play are dimensions of life that belong together. This makes sense of the linguistic and historical connection between holy days and holidays, and between the important theological, redemptive concepts of play and re-creation. Holidays (when one plays) are derived from holy days (sabbath days, Sundays and festival days) and the connection is not merely one of convenience (such that a day without work can be utilized as a day when one plays) but it is intrinsic to the nature of the holy day. One plays on holidays not simply because one has time but because that is one of the main points of the holy day. When, after years of neglect of the Scriptures, the Israelites gathered to hear Ezra read the book of the law of Moses it became clear that they had failed in many ways, but Ezra's answer to their despair was that because this was now a holy day—for they had heard the words of the law—they should not be grieved but should go home and "enjoy choice food and sweet wine" and "to celebrate with great joy, because they now understood the words that had been made known to them" (Neh 8:1–12). Holy days and festivals were to be times of joy and delight, involving feasting and fun and even dance. This connection between work, rest and play is something that is often lost in the life of the church, which is a tragedy as play takes one's relationship with God beyond doing, having and achieving and takes one into enjoying, appreciating and sharing. It emphasizes the creative life rather than merely the productive one and the aesthetic life rather than simply the ethical one. In the life of the redeemed play is an element of both work and rest. It is important to work, because without it work is drudgery, and important to rest, because without it rest is simply passivity. Play makes work and rest the delight that they ought to be.

Playing with the Idea of Play

Playing with Work and Creativity

This chapter discusses work and play. Assuming that "work" refers to whatever your main occupation in life is, whether paid employment, parenting, retirement or whatever, can you see your work in terms of play? While doing your work fully and well how can you have more play, more fun, more creativity? Could your work be done better if there was more of these things? In what way do you see work and play in relationship to God? How can you enrich those you work with through play, fun and creativity?

7

Love: Play and True Beauty

Let him kiss me with the kisses of his mouth.

—THE SHULAMITE WOMAN (SONG OF SOLOMON 1:2)

After hearing me speak enthusiastically about having visited several churches in Germany that had stained glass windows by the early modernist artist Marc Chagall, a friend lent me a copy of the Bible that was illustrated exclusively with reproductions of his work. But it was a slightly unusual edition as it only contained three of the books of the Bible: Genesis, Exodus and the Song of Solomon.[1] "That's a somewhat limited sort of Bible", I commented somewhat wryly, "though I suppose it has the essentials!"

It is somewhat doubtful, however, that many would include the sexy love song of Solomon in a list of "The Three (*or even the Ten*) Most Essential Books of the Bible." But even though it probably wouldn't rate highly it nonetheless fulfills an important function within the canon of Scripture in that it is a constant reminder of the intimacy, the passion, the playfulness and even the sexuality and sensuality involved in a relationship with God. (And when one puts it that way it is possible to perhaps see, bearing in mind the common rather sober attitude of many Christians, why it has *not* achieved great favor with everyone!) In this unusual book one hears the murmurings of two lovers:

> Let him kiss me with the kisses of his mouth—for your love is more delightful than wine . . . no wonder the young women love you . . . Take me away with you . . . your cheeks are beautiful . . .

1. Chagall, *Bible*.

your neck . . . your breasts . . . your eyes . . . your teeth . . . all
beautiful you are, my darling; there is no flaw in you . . . my lover
is resting between my breasts . . . you have stolen my heart . . . I
have taken off my robe . . . my heart began to pound . . . I opened
for my lover . . . you are like the palm . . . I will climb the palm tree
and take hold of its fruit . . . let us spend the night in the village . . .
place me like a seal over your heart.

Physical love is, of course, intrinsically playful. Erotic love begins with
"foreplay" and it would be highly offensive if one's amorous advances were
interpreted as work or duty rather than as play and pleasure. Sexual relations
without playfulness is not love, which has to be free, joyful and playful, and
this is what one finds in the Song of Solomon. But the use of erotic, playful
love as an image of relationship with God has always been somewhat problematic. On the one hand, it has appeared to be too earthly and physical, and
too unspiritual for use as a suitable model for a relationship with God. But
on the other hand, a relationship characterized by fervent feelings, extreme
ardor, unbridled enthusiasm, extreme zeal and great delight is a wonderful
thing and *ought* to be seen as part of our relationship with God. And then,
in a slightly more controversial addition, it is also the case that our understanding of God's love for the world should not be entirely stripped of the
passionate or even, in a metaphorical sense, the erotic. Whether the Song
of Solomon is best understood in historical, dramatic, cultic or allegorical
terms it is, at the very least, clear that erotic sensuality was seen by the writer,
and by those responsible for the development of the canon of Scripture, as
an appropriate means of expressing a significant truth about the nature of
the human-divine relationship. The book is full of playfulness, fun, sexual
desire, pleasure, delight, teasing, dance, surprise, celebration, ecstasy and joy
and it affirms the essential goodness and joy of sensual, playful love. Rather
than being embarrassed by the physicality of the Song of Solomon the playful love it promotes should be front and center as part of kingdom life. In
"Theology and the Playful Life" Lewis Smedes wrote,

> The sexual component of our nature testifies that man was meant
> to find the most meaningful human communion in a playful rela-
> tionship. In mutual trust and loving commitment, sexual activity
> is to be a playful festivity. It attests that human being is closest to
> fulfilling itself in a game. To be in God's image, then, includes be-
> ing sexual, and sexuality is a profound call to play.[2]

2. Smedes, "Theology and the Playful Life," 59.

Jesus and the Woman at the Well

Although physical, sexual play is certainly at the heart of the Song of Solomon an explicit connection between sexuality and spirituality is not common in biblical material. There is, however, a subtle play on the spiritual and physical love between a man and a woman in John's account of Jesus' meeting with the woman of Samaria. This encounter, as we shall see, is presented in a romantic context although it has a spiritual meaning. While it is not to be interpreted in the crude, physical sense that is sometimes suggested of the relationship between Jesus and Mary Magdalene, where some have seen them as married or otherwise sexually engaged, the significance of the passion, love and intimacy that is hinted at in the story of the woman of Samaria is not to be overlooked.

The most common interpretations of Jesus' meeting with the woman of Samaria (John 4:1–30) stress the point that Jesus was willing to talk to, and accept, a Samaritan, but the subtext of this narrative goes much further and points to Jesus being, in a spiritual but nonetheless passionate sense, her lover. To be able to discern this it is necessary for the contemporary reader to consider what a typical Jewish listener of the first century would have known about the stories of Abraham, Isaac, Jacob, Moses, David and the other ancient heroes of the faith before coming to this particular account of Jesus meeting the woman. These ancient stories of the patriarchs were essentially "family history" and would have been told and retold many times and, in an era when there was a marked absence of television and novels, they were entertainment as well as religious authority. One might well imagine that the exciting stories of battle and warfare, the suspenseful accounts of deceit and intrigue and the romantic stories of love and loss would have been particularly popular. The people of Jesus' day were, of course, familiar with the literary conventions of the various genres of writing and storytelling found in the Scriptures. That is, they understood the differences between and the subtleties of poetry, proverb, historical narrative, romance and so forth, in just the same way that modern people are familiar with the conventions for thrillers, crime stories, police dramas and so on in literature, film and television today. It is of considerable significance that John's account of the meeting of the woman of Samaria and Jesus clearly follows one ancient Jewish formulaic pattern of romantic love stories based around meetings at wells. There was a pattern for these stories that was as well established as the ones that exist in certain types of television series today.

The basic plot formula for these well stories is quite straightforward, and follows, with variation for dramatic effect, the following outline:

1. A young Jewish man goes on a journey,

2. into foreign territory,

3. in order to find a suitable, Jewish wife.

4. He stops at a well (the local meeting place),

5. where he meets a beautiful young woman,

6. who provides him (and/or his flock) with water.

7. Something happens that is unusual (for example, the girl needs help fighting off the local bullies or they discover long-lost family connections),

8. they engage in conversation,

9. and then the woman runs off to tell everyone about the young man she has just met.

10. Naturally, love and marriage follow on.

In essence, this is what happens in no less than four bible stories involving Isaac and Rebekah, Jacob and Rachel, Moses and Zipporah and, of course, Jesus and the woman of Samaria.

A brief recounting of the similarities and the all-important variations, between these will help establish the main point. The story of Isaac and Rebekah (Gen 24:1–69) begins with Abraham getting old while his son, Isaac, remains unmarried. They are living in Cannaanite territory and Abraham is determined that Isaac would *not* marry a Cannaanite so he sends one of his servants on a journey to the city where Nahor, Abraham's brother, lives, in order to find a wife for Isaac. The servant goes to the well and prays that the first girl he asks to help him get a drink will be "the one you have chosen for your servant Isaac." Rebekah comes and the text notes that "she was very beautiful." He asks for a drink and she not only provides this but also helps water his camels. The servant is ecstatic to discovers that not only is she a Jew but she is related to Abraham. Here is a hard-working, beautiful Jewish girl already distantly related who comes as an answer to a very direct prayer! Rebekah then runs to tell her mother's household all about these things. Isaac, of course, ends up not only marrying her but, it is specifically pointed out, loving her very much as well. Note that this fulfills all of the ten characteristics of a well romance noted above, providing that one notes a dramatic variation in that there is a servant who acts as a proxy for Isaac.

Isaac, in his turn, does not want his son Jacob to marry a Canaanite (Gen 28–29), so in similar fashion he sends Jacob to uncle Laban to find a wife and true love. Jacob comes to his tribal home and to a well that is later named after him, where he meets Rachel. In this case it is Jacob who helps Rachel water her sheep and when he discovers that they are related he is overcome with emotion. Rebekah, it is specifically noted in the text, like Rachel runs off to tell people about what has happened. And, of course, they fall in love and marry. The story follows the standard pattern except for the fact that although Jacob travels through foreign lands he ends up in what might be considered to be home territory.

Moses, for his part, was fleeing from Pharaoh after killing a slave when he ends up at a well in Midian (Exod 2). There he meets not merely one girl but the seven daughters of Jethro, the priest of Midian, including Zipporah. While the sisters re filling the troughs to water their father's flock some shepherds come along and drive them away, but Moses comes to their rescue and waters their flock for them. After that the story specifically notes that they have to rush off to tell their father about their hero. He rebukes them for leaving him at the well and he takes Moses into his house and ends up giving him Zipporah as his wife. In this case the significant variation is that Zipporah is not Jewish but a Midianite.

Jewish readers listening to John's gospel knew these stories by heart and so when they realized that they were hearing an account of a young man meeting a woman at a well they would have had no doubts about what might well eventuate! And, in this case, they might have been shocked by the implications as well! John's gospel provides a careful and detailed account of the meeting between Jesus and the woman of Samaria and it is presented to his Jewish listeners complete with all the characteristics of a story about love at the local well. Notice the details by which John makes this absolutely clear: a young man, Jesus, meets a woman at a well; it is specifically noted that this is foreign territory, Samaria; there is a discussion about water; then there is talk about marriage; the woman is astounded at what Jesus tells her and after their conversation runs excitedly into town to tell everyone about the astonishing things that have happened.

And in case the connection between this encounter and the ancient well stories is still not clear John makes it blindingly obvious by giving his readers two other clues. Firstly, he points out that although this took place in foreign territory it was at none other than *Jacob's* well, where one of the previous romantic encounters had happened. Get the hint? And, secondly, he makes sure that this meeting of Jesus and the woman of Samaria follows on immediately after an account of John the Baptist telling his disciples that he, John, was not the Christ but only the best man (as we would say today) *who goes ahead of the groom to make sure that everything is ready for the wedding* (John 3:25–30). In short, with these words the scene is now set for the arrival of the groom, which takes place in the following story as the narrative moves on to describe Jesus coming to meet with the Samaritan woman. The gospel writer really could not do any more to make it clearer that Jesus is to be understood as a lover seeking his beloved, a bridegroom seeking a bride.

Understanding this meeting of Jesus and the woman of Samaria in terms of ancient, romantic well stories means taking a somewhat playful interpretation with Jesus seen as lover and future husband. When Jesus goes to the well he intends to take this woman in spiritual marriage. Perhaps this is presented in a subtle, non-explicit way because it was a message that would have been too radical for some. But it is a case of "whoever has ears, let them hear" (Matt 11:15). This is an enacted parable about God's love for his people.

This romantic story may not be as explicit as the Song of Solomon but it is more playful than, for example, the formal language about Christ and his bride in Ephesians (5:22–33). In the way that John presents his account of the woman meeting Jesus he is playing with his readers and listeners, challenging them to see more in this meeting that might initially be apparent.

Using a set formula, whether in literature or film, has certain advantages. Those familiar with them can appreciate the detail with which a particular story is built up, and they will have a heightened sense of anticipation because they know, at least in part, what is going to happen. But the best part always comes when the story breaks away from the expected pattern and suddenly moves in new and unfamiliar ways. And in this case, for the typical Jewish listener familiar with well stories, the meeting of Jesus with the woman of Samaria contains a number of such surprises.

The Idea of the Beautiful

In the ancient well stories Rebekah, Rachel and Zipporah are all young, single, virginal and beautiful and they come to the well to meet their lover. Of course, they do not know that is what they are doing but the reader waits with great anticipation for this to happen! It is said of Rebekah that "the girl was very beautiful, a virgin, no man had ever lain with her (Gen 24:16)" and Rachel was so beautiful that when Jacob saw her he went to her immediately and always loved her deeply (29:9–30). But nothing like this could be said of the woman of Samaria. She has previously had five husbands and, as Jesus points out, the one she now has is not really hers. She is no beauty. And she is certainly not virginal. After five, possibly six, failed relationships she would have to be considered well past her prime. But the woman wants to avoid any discussion of this and after declaring that Jesus must be a prophet she quickly moves on to another topic, about where one ought to worship.

But the astute reader or listener will observe that the number of husbands she has had is significant for two reasons. Firstly, it tells us a lot about her life. After six husbands it is not only unlikely that she is not young or as beautiful as she was as a young girl, but one might also think that someone who has had six husbands is probably a person with a lot of psychological and social issues. It is difficult to think that she has much self-respect or much esteem in the community. She may well have been the victim of serial abuse from husbands who divorced her. Or she may have suffered from abuse in her earlier background and she may have a personality disorder. We cannot know the detail or the causes but there is very little doubt that she is a damaged and vulnerable person. But she is the one in Samaria that Jesus loves.

The second reason the number of husbands is significant is because of the number itself. In John's gospel numbers can be symbolic, like the six jars of water at the wedding at Cana and the seven "I am" sayings.[3] Six represents something that is incomplete, unfinished because it is one short of the perfection, the fullness, the completion that is represented by the number seven. And so the story opens up to a new possibility. She has had six husbands, none of whom are her real husband; will there be another? A seventh? And now, of course, she is meeting a man at a well, as did Rebekah, Rachel and Zipporah. Could Jesus be the perfect seventh? The husband

---

3. John 2:6; 6:35; 8:12; 10:7; 10:11; 11:25; 14:6; 15:1.

who will truly love her? These are the questions raised for Jewish listener by the way the story is presented.

The most common interpretation of the story of the woman of Samaria is that Jesus challenged the division between Jews and Samaritans, and there is absolutely no doubt that this is important. But when the story is seen in the context of the other well stories the particular situation of this woman—in sharp contrast to that of the women in the other stories—comes to the fore. The radical message that is found here is that Jesus loves the damaged and the brokenhearted; he cares for the unbeautiful of the world, the abused woman, the damaged, the excluded and the rejected. And this is not only theory; it is something seen in a touching and very personal way.

The grace and love that Jesus shows to the woman transforms her life. John carefully notes that she immediately goes—as all the women at the wells do—and tells others about what has happened. In her case, she tells everyone! She goes and says, "Come see a man who has told me everything I have ever done." Saying that is a risk for someone with a history like hers! It could draw out some cruel and crude responses. But her willingness to be vulnerable and her enthusiasm means that what is good news for her also becames good news for the town as well ("Many of the Samaritans from that town believed in him because of the woman's testimony"). So the Samaritans urge him to stay with them and he stays two days, "and because of his words many more became believers. They said to the woman, 'We no longer believe just because of what you said; now we have heard for ourselves, and we know that this man really is the Savior of the world.'" (4:39–42). Jesus' love changes her life and she becomes a missionary to her own town. Because she is loved she is able to love and witness to others. One can only speculate on how it changed her life in the long term and what it meant for social relationships within the town. The woman of Samaria might not have been beautiful as the world reckons beauty but in Christ's eyes she was indeed beautiful. The subtle challenge to the listener to this story is to see the contrast and to consider what it means that Jesus loved this woman. He became her lover, her true husband.

Perhaps the overarching point is that in every age people need to engage in ministry as excited lovers, with the enthusiasm and passion that she displayed. The gospel comes to the broken and the damaged and those who learn that they are loved are empowered to be able to love others. Indeed, only those who know they are loved can show love to another. And the story of the love between Jesus and the woman of Samaria is only one example of a love that continues today.

A Modern Woman of Samaria

I first met Angie when she and her partner were referred to me from a local municipal welfare worker who asked if the church could provide them with some food and some financial help. The message was that they needed help but also that they had a tendency to be somewhat manipulative, and their relationship was tenuous. Indeed, it was not long before Angie's partner disappeared from the scene completely. It was clear that Angie had innumerable problems. Physically she was unwell and overweight—when she came to see me I seriously feared that the chair she sat on might not hold her; she had constant pain from an ankle injury; she had other, ongoing medical problems; she alternated between passiveness and aggression; she was incapable of running finances or her life; she was emotionally unstable; she had used drugs and her school-aged daughter had been taken away from her by welfare authorities. She was on some serious prescription medication to help her, and she lived in a single room in an accommodation house primarily designed for workers at a nearby mine.

In the first, and what I thought would be the only, meeting with her she and her partner received food and some money. For me it was a difficult pastoral meeting because one does not want to give any suggestion that the food and money is given conditionally—it is given freely to anyone in need. But at the same time it can be a failure of witness not to say something about the reason that Christians care for people. It can even be hypocritical if it means allowing people to think that one is good in one's own strengthen and as the result of one's own initiative, rather than giving credit to God who calls and enables. In any event, I think that the actual words I did say about it were not as relevant as the fact that the Holy Spirit was speaking to her. The following day she surprised me by ringing and asking to see me in order to talk more about God. We did this and I gave her a Bible and suggested she read Luke's gospel, not really expecting much. But when I returned a few days later she had not only read Luke but most of Acts and she had a notebook with a long list of questions about what she had read. "What," she asked as one her many questions, "is an apostle?" She had never come across the word before. I did my best with a brief explanation and she immediately declared, "Well, you are my apostle." And thereafter she wanted me to guide her in every area of life. It became quite difficult to get her to reduce those expectations and to sidestep getting involved in inappropriate areas of her life and to find other people to help her. Despite all her problems Angie was a very intelligent and articulate person who not only felt completely unloved but also abused and rejected. She became a committed follower of Jesus and set about changing her life. Many people became involved in this and saw the changes that came into her life, the passion with which she was a follower and the commitment she now had. This challenged and impressed many people. When I looked up at the congregation after baptizing her I saw a whole congregation in tears.

Angie wanted to be able to get her child back and she also wanted to become a full-time ordained minister. She insisted on having a long-range plan that included this. I insisted that there were many other things that had to happen first, some of which would take some time, but she set herself a goal of achieving this in six years or so. As part of her plans to reestablish contact with her daughter she moved right across the country, reconnected with her, associated with a church there and continued to change. Then, just months later, I received a phone call to say that she was dead. It was, unsurprisingly, a difficult and unclear situation. I was given different accounts of her death, one involved a car accident, another a drug overdose. In one sense it was a tragic end to what had become a powerful story of redemption but in another sense it was not really unexpected.

Humanly speaking, Angie had been an unattractive, overweight, unwell, passive-aggressive who had significant health, personal and social problems. Spiritually, just like the woman of Samaria, Jesus saw her as a beautiful virgin that he loved very much. And Angie knew, and now would always know, the love of Jesus in her life. For the first time she had been able to really show love to others because she had received love herself. In the end, Angie could not completely overcome her problems in this world, and while we know nothing of the subsequent life of the woman of Samaria the story of Angie stands as a reminder that there is no guarantee that everything will be fine and easy for Christians.

The stories of the woman of Samaria and Angie are more down-to-earth and realistic that the typical romantic love story, but precisely because of this they are able to demonstrate even more powerfully the great love of God shown in the life and ministry of Jesus.

A Playful Story

Notice that the woman of Samaria, unlike Nicodemus—the central figure in the previous story—is not named. Anonymity is not unusual in John's gospel; it seems to be a feature of his writing for he has a number of stories about unnamed people, including the lame man by the pool, the woman caught in adultery, the man born blind and the official in Capernaum who begged Jesus to heal his son, as well as the woman of Samaria and, even more unusually, "the mother of Jesus" (rather than "Mary") and "the beloved disciple" (rather than "John"?).[4] Indeed, Nicodemus is an exception, perhaps because people would not have believed that a Pharisee would come by night to be instructed by Jesus. (We can imagine early listeners saying, "Oh, yes, Nicodemus, we know he followed Jesus!") Generally though, it is as though the name does not matter, perhaps in order to emphasize that they represent different groups of people. This unnamed Samaritan woman is representative of all Samaritans—they are all being invited to a spiritual marriage, to take on a spiritual husband.

The Samaritans were the descendants of those Jews who married Assyrians after the fall of the Northern Kingdom hundreds of years previously. They were considered traitors by other Jews. Another point of difference was that although the Samaritans worshipped the God of Israel they rejected Jerusalem as the center of worship. believing that Mt. Gerazim was more holy. As a result, John notes, "Jews do not associate with Samaritans" (4:9). Jesus' acceptance of Samaritans in general, as well as the woman herself, is confirmed by Jesus' response when the woman shifts the conversation away from her own marital status by asking about the right place to worship. Jesus begins with a critical word by saying, "You Samaritans worship what you do not know; we worship what we do know, for salvation is from the Jews." But he then moves on to bridge the gap between Jew and Samaritan by referring to a future time when neither Jerusalem nor Gerazim will be the place of worship but all true worshippers "will worship the Father in spirit and in truth" (4:23). In these words, as well as in his attitude towards the woman, he is making it clear that the barriers between Jew and Samaritan are gone.

Becoming involved with a Samaritan woman was a serious departure from both the cultural norm of the day and the well story formula but, it must be noted, it is one that has a precedent in the story of Moses. He

---

4. John 5:5; 8:53; 9:1; 4:46; 4:7.

was fleeing for his life from dangerous territory—Egypt—when he came to Midian. Significantly for the story, in some respects the Midianites sat in a similar situation to Samaritans. That is, they were also alienated relations, in their case descendants of Midian, the son of Abraham, but the tribe to whom Joseph's brothers sold him into slavery (Gen 37:28). And, like the Samaritans, they may have had different worship practices as a result of their close association with the Ishmaelites and Moabites. Nonetheless, Moses found acceptance and a home with them, and married Zipporah. In short, he married outside the family, and one might wonder whether this precedent, by such a notable hero of the faith, might not have caused some young men with an eye for a foreign girl to argue with their parents, "Well, if Moses could marry a Midianite, why can't I?"

Judaism, however, strongly resisted this kind of intermarriage but, for Christians, when Jesus showed love to a Samaritan woman the barrier that Moses initially crossed was broken down for all time. Samaritans are invited into the kingdom. Jesus' redefinition of those to be considered beautiful is only deepened and made more significant by the fact that the woman was not Jewish but Samaritan.

In the story of the woman of Samaria John is engaging in a playful way of teaching his readers and listeners. It requires the reader to understand a particular tradition, be able to discern a subtle underlying message and draw spiritual conclusions based on a series of romantic stories. The process is similar to what happens in the interpretation of a parable, though in this case the stories are found within historical narrative. The fundamental point that Jesus accepts Samaritans would be obvious on almost any reading of the text but a playful, romantic interpretation allows for an even deeper understanding of his intentions. The message is clear: God's love is for all, even—perhaps especially—for those alienated from us and those who might be considered enemies. Jesus is the great Lover who perfectly and completely fulfills the natural human desire for the beautiful, but he redefines what is beautiful to include those who are damaged and rejected. And he crosses boundaries to embrace those usually excluded. His love does not come in the form of a principle of a philosophy but can be seen in actual practice in his wooing of the Samaritan woman. It is a concrete example of what it means to "love your enemies."

Playing with the Idea of Play

Playing with the Physical and the Beautiful

This chapter looks at the relationship between play and love, sexuality, physicality, truth, beauty, and relationships. It suggests, among other things, that love is playful, that play is often physical (although the physical is rarely seen as being related to the spiritual), that truth is both beautiful and playful, and that relationships develop through play. Do something physical to enhance your relationships with God or others. It might involve doing something physically caring (something that involves your body rather than your mind or your money) or expressing yourself creatively (in a way that you have not done before, creating something that has no other purpose than to bring beauty—however modest—into being) or being physically loving (in ways appropriate to the other person involved). Note that, for our purposes here, it does not count if it is primarily seen as a Christian responsibility rather than as fun, play, and pleasure. Afterwards, reflect on what it means to do something like this.

8

Redemption: Play and Pain

Who is there, for instance, in our times, who can devote himself
with an easy mind to music, friendship, games, or happiness?
Surely not the "ethical" man, but only the Christian.

—DIETRICH BONHOEFFER[1]

I t was in a letter written in January 1944, while imprisoned by the Nazis
in Tegel prison, that Bonhoeffer made the above reflection on the way
one ought to live in the mist of the most difficult times one can imagine.
Of course, given the dire circumstances, Bonhoeffer was careful to nuance
his position. He distinguished genuine Christian happiness from false
bravado, and he did not avoid the moral responsibilities for action that
the war brought. But he repudiated the view that people are happy as the
result of play, and was insistent that friendship, play, music and happiness
all emerge from an attitude of trust in God. For Bonhoeffer, it is only the
Christian who can play in the midst of desperate danger, pain and suffering
because the Christian life is fundamentally lived within God, embraced *in*
Christ. He did not see play, music or friendship as the *means* to happiness;
rather they are the *result* of a relationship with God. Nor are repression,
imprisonment or war factors that can prevent the Christian—but only the
Christian—from engaging in games or music because the Christian attitude is not based on mere circumstances.

This is the result of Trinitarian theology, through which the believer
is more than an observer of divinity or one who relates externally to God
but becomes one who lives *within* God, a participant in Trinitarian life.

1. Bonhoeffer, *Letters and Papers from Prison*, 59.

As Catherine LaCugna says, "The life of God—precisely because God is Triune—does not belong to God alone."[2] The divine life is also *our* life, and play—as an intrinsically engaging and joyful activity—expresses this interactive dynamic more effectively than any other metaphor. An understanding like this means that when one is faced with the kind of difficulties Bonhoeffer faced then one's own strength and abilities become irrelevant and the *essential task* is to learn to trust in being in God's hands. And once one has done that it becomes possible to live!

Bonhoeffer's approach to the relationship between pain and play reveals the importance of having these concepts in the right order. While there is an element of truth in the notion that playing more, or developing a more playful attitude, leads to a fuller or more enhancing spiritual life, this is *not* the primary point. The suggestion that doing a bit less work and playing a few more games is the secret to a strong spiritual life runs the risk of trivializing the matter. No, the real order of things is precisely the reverse—that a rich spiritual life leads one to play, and to all that is involved in a playful attitude to life, including contentment in all situations, complete trust in God, the absence of worry and despair and the presence of joy and happiness despite the problem of all kinds of pain.

The Problem of Pain

The problem of *pain*, which Bonhoeffer addresses, is also the problem of *play*. The pain of the world in all its various aspects, extending from the dramatic to the ordinary and from the extreme to the trivial, produces two reactions in regard to play. For some, such as Bonhoeffer's friend who had made this point about pain, it becomes difficult and inappropriate to play at all, while others, who do not apparently feel this way, can play *too much* and their play becomes obsessive and dysfunctional. This form of inauthentic play, which abounds in the contemporary world, emerges as a release from unsatisfying work or as a means to ignore other painful realities, whether local or global. This form of play has a tendency to become self-centered, rather than genuinely communal, and a substitute for the authentic freedom that play represents. The ultimate inadequacy of this form of play means that it tends to become addictive and introverted, and this provides an opportunity for others to take advantage of this fact, and the play is frequently sexualized and commercialized. The issue here—of

2. LaCugna, *God for Us*, 1.

distorting that which is good and healthy—is easily observed, and is something that Augustine reflected on in his *Confessions*. He observes that as a child he was led astray by the love of playing and then, as an adult, by the pleasures of food. His main discussion of the dangers of pleasure, and the way one can become captive to it, is undertaken in respect of food and drink, rather than play, but his observations are equally relevant. Even though these are natural needs, he says, he controls his eating and drinking precisely because he finds pleasure in them, and it is so easy to become addicted to them and focused on these pleasures rather than upon God. Pleasure is a danger and so "I fight against it, for fear of becoming its captive." He finds in eating and drinking "an ominous kind of enjoyment" whereby the danger is not in pleasure as such but in becoming captive to it. He is well aware of the deceptiveness of the human heart, and regretfully notes that it is difficult to determine precisely what is needed for health and what is taken purely for pleasure: "my unhappy soul welcomes this uncertainty, using it to vindicate and excuse itself. It is glad that the proper requirements of health are in doubt, so that under the pretense of caring for health it may disguise the pursuit of pleasure." Augustine is certainly right that we must not become addicted to eating or drinking, or to the pursuit of pleasure in other ways, and he does recognize that eating and drinking and so forth are gifts from God, but he does not allow himself to be truly grateful for them, and to enjoy them for what they are, beyond what is necessary for good health. His zeal for avoiding addiction, his daily struggle against greed, did not allow him to appreciate or enjoy them or find in this world any "foretaste" of heavenly joy.[3]

It is now possible to see the irony of the fact that play is seen as inappropriate for very different reasons. The discussion of Bonhoeffer shows that some argue that the presence of *pain* in the world makes play impossible, while the discussion of Augustine shows that others say that it is the danger inherent in the *pleasure* of play that does it. Thus play is rejected because of both pleasure and pain. But the answer to these twin problems is not, as many suggest, the rejection of play, but rather an acceptance of the proper role of play as an integral part of both the mission and the goal of the church of Jesus Christ. That is, play is part of the redemptive *mission* of the church in that a playful spirituality and a joyful communal life are intrinsic to the process of the transformation of the world. At the same time, play is an important part of the eschatological *goal* towards which all things are

3. Augustine, *Confessions*, 1.10 and 10.31.

directed. Play is one of the most profound metaphors of life in the future kingdom of God. In this way there is a congruence of mission and goal, of means and end, in the redemption achieved through Christ. This is one element of the way that Christ is both the means of salvation—the ultimate revelation and the redeemer—and the goal, the end, the purpose of salvation—that all things find their meaning in him.

It is important to see play as a form of the mission of the church. Christians are those who have truly been made free, and play is an illustration of the liberation of humanity from sin and death and all forms of bondage. Living in this way means demonstrating a different form of lifestyle and a radically different approach to understanding the world. To those without understanding it appears to be the way of the fool or the clown because it involves a fundamentally different way of seeing things, but to the Christian it is the true wisdom of God. The apostle Paul, for example, plays with the way people understood his imprisonment. After years languishing in jail in Jerusalem under governors Felix and Festus, and then in Rome under the emperor, it was clear that he was, for all intents and purposes, a prisoner of Caesar, yet in writing from his cell he describes himself to the Ephesians as "a prisoner of Christ Jesus" (3:1), thus expressing an ability to understand things as they really were rather than as they appeared to be to others. He and the other believers were living—as one does when one is playing—within the existing world according to a different set of rules, with a different perception of what was real. This is no trivial form of playing but a way of life that is both serious and joyful. It is a way of life that is illustrative of the future life of the kingdom of God; that is, the kingdom has come and *is present* in this living.

The language of play is important because it indicates clearly the ethos of the community of Christ. It stresses the joyful, interactive, intimate, communal nature of life together, and challenges any view of the kingdom that excludes fun, laughter, games, creativity, dance or joy. This is the way of life that Christians and the church are to present to the world. Of course, given the discussion above, it should be clear that this form of life does not mean the *avoidance* of pain or suffering, although it does transform one's attitude towards them. As one can see in what Bonhoeffer said, play and pain are not mutually exclusive. Playfulness does not itself banish all pain, but nor does the presence of pain mean an immediate end to play or pleasure. In the church's demonstration of kingdom life in the present age, pain and play coincide until the time comes when pain is banished and suffering ceases: "Look! God's dwelling place is now among the people, and he will dwell with them. They will be his people, and God himself will be with them and be their God. 'He will wipe every tear from their eyes. There will be no more death' or mourning or crying or pain, for the old order of things has passed away" (Rev 21:3–4). And so, on the one hand, in the present age pain and suffering remain, albeit temporarily, and those who believe in the alternate reality of the kingdom of God must deal with them, but, on the other hand, some things should immediately be banished from this alternate reality, including boredom, dullness, listlessness and tedium, because these are attitudes to life that are intrinsically contrary to the life of Christ's new kingdom.

The Why of Salvation

Understanding the life of the kingdom in terms of play is helpful and important but also somewhat unusual because traditionally the focus has fallen on other aspects of soteriology. The Western theological tradition has stressed the necessity of the incarnation as a remedy for human sin. Redemption is interpreted in terms of the way that the effects of sin are undone. This focus on the remedy for sin makes it clear *why* God had to become man—in order to save people from their sin—but it does not explain why God *wanted* to become man.

Anselm's famous question, *Cur Deus Homo* ("Why [did] God [become] Man?"), has been profoundly important for Western Christianity; it has set the agenda and framed subsequent discussions. Anselm's own interpretation of the answer to this question was expressed in terms of the necessary satisfaction of divine honor, while later the Reformers saw the atonement in judicial terms, as a satisfaction of divine justice. But the way the question is framed is important as it determines the way the discussion proceeds. Satisfaction theories, such as those of Anselm and the Reformers, work with the concept of necessity, but how does one understand the idea that God feels some kind of need to save humanity? Surely from God's perspective there is no *need* to do anything. Yet, nonetheless, God does it and, because there can be no external requirement placed on God, this inevitably says something about the inner character of God. Similarly, if soteriology is framed in judicial terms, with God as judge and the Son as the one who brings justification, then this will inevitably also influence one's understanding of the divine attributes. But the questions can be framed differently and the question "Why did Christ die for our sins?" is not the only one that can be asked. Even if one answers the question regarding the necessity for Christ's death if humanity is to be saved, one can still also ask the question, "Why would God *want* to do this?" What is it that lies behind the divine desire to defeat sin and to be prepared to undergo all that was necessary to bring about salvation? The answer is obviously related to the love that God has for humanity, but even then the question can be asked about what it is that divine love seeks to achieve and the reason that God has in showing this great love. In pursuing these questions one ultimately goes beyond those good, healing, salvific and necessary answers that emerge from consideration of the cross of Christ, and one comes to the joy and the freedom that come from the resurrection. The ultimate reason for the incarnation is found in the resurrection life, the joy and laughter of the redeemed. Redemption is nothing other than the restoration of human freedom, the freedom to play and rejoice in the presence of God. In the cross there is salvation and healing and atonement for sin, but with the resurrection there is the joy and laughter of the community of the redeemed.

One might sometimes wonder whether in this world there are not more important things to do than play, but then when one considers the nature of redeemed life as a time of playful, joyful intimacy with Christ, one might wonder whether there is *anything* more important than seeking to make this joyful future a reality in the present.

Crucifixion as Play

While the connection between play and the resurrection life is relatively easy to discern, the idea that the cross of Christ can also be interpreted in the light of play is less obvious. Indeed, for Jürgen Moltmann in *The Theology of Play* it was the reality of the cross that, for him, made the imagery of play problematic.[4] This issue was, however, directly addressed by Robert E. Neale in "The Crucifixion as Play." Neale makes the point that although it may seem as though play and song and dance do not fit a theological interpretation of the suffering and death of the cross, this is perhaps because play has been thought of in superficial terms. Play is commonly thought of in terms of pleasure and fun, as a lightweight, non-essential diversion from the other, more substantial and genuinely important dimensions of life. But an understanding of play that assumes that play is only a lightweight, trivial

4. Moltmann, *Theology of Play*, 28.

pursuit, involving only happy feelings and undertaken simply to provide pleasure and a relief from the more serious dimensions of life, is a fundamentally inadequate understanding of what is, in reality, a multifaceted, significant and profound human and divine experience.

Of course, play does have those lightweight dimensions but it is also a form of life that extends to much greater depths. Even the ordinary human experience of play has a depth to it that can point towards the appropriateness of play as a way of understanding the crucifixion. This depth is seen in the way in which play is agonistic, risky, passionate and purposeful. For play theorist Johan Huizinga the *agonistic* or combative dimension is *the* key element of play, and the challenge it involves is not to be interpreted in trivial terms. The development of the person depends upon it. The essential competitive, combative nature of much play—both mental and physical—and its relational dimension was discussed earlier,[5] where it was shown to be a process that tests one's capacities and provides an opportunity for one to develop. This includes the psychological development that comes with the need to deal with unknown and unpredictable outcomes, and with both success and failure. Play is thus a serious business in life, and it can be, at its highest levels, both difficult and stressful. It may be challenging because of the external circumstances or because of one's internal expectations, hopes and fears. Being an Olympian means taking the playing of games to the highest physical and emotional level; it can be painful in various ways and it involves much in terms of time, effort, energy and commitment. It can also be extremely risky. The cultural tendency now, however, is to minimize the competitive dimension and to reduce the risk involved in it. By and large we are a risk-averse society, and so most games are carefully monitored and controlled to ensure complete safety. Indeed, a game or an adventure that involves too much risk is modified or stopped. Yet in many games there remains an element of risk simply because it is intrinsic to the playing. Those used to less risky endeavors tend to stop seeing an activity with too much risk as play and regard it as foolishness. But for others it is essential, even when it is distressing or foolish to others. Mountaineering, around-the-world solo yacht racing, wingsuit flying and ski jumping all terrify me but they simply constitute challenging play for others. Personally, I see sufficient risk and challenge in sailing single- and double-handed small boats— having to deal with being on the water by oneself, the risk involved in

5. See chapter 4.

overturning the boat and concerns about one's own and others' safety in rough weather. Of course, many of these concerns could have been alleviated in various ways or even eliminated by not sailing at particular times, but pushing the boundaries, going to the limit to see how far one can go is, precisely the point of the exercise! By putting oneself in such positions it is possible to ascertain and experience the limits of one's mental and physical capabilities, and if one doesn't want that then on doesn't have to do it. Nonetheless, the risks in both real life and fantasy playing can be extreme and do not necessarily exclude the possibility of death—either real or imagined. Game playing allows for personal consideration of the possibility of death, either in fantasy and imagination or in risk taking and sometimes, tragically, in reality. In this way it is similar to descriptions of risk and death in film and literature—they enable us to understand something of ourselves and the world in which we live. Games may be fun but they can, at the same time, deal with very serious issues of life. Consequently, the play metaphor is not necessarily frivolous or inappropriate when considering either the life of Christ and his death on the cross or the life and destiny of any human being.

The spiritual parallels with games are obvious, and are expressed in various biblical passages including Paul's exhortation to the Corinthians, "Do you not know that in a race the runners all compete, but only one receives the prize? Run in such a way as to get the prize. Everyone who competes in the games goes into strict training. They do it to get a crown that will not last, but we do it to get a crown that will last forever. Therefore I do not run like someone running aimlessly; I do not fight like a boxer beating the air" (1 Cor 9:24–26).

The agonistic element of Christ's life, and of the Christian life in general, is essential not only spiritually but also soteriologically, although in popular Western evangelical piety the soteriological dimension is understated. The tendency is to emphasize the—undoubtedly central—action of the death of Christ on the cross in isolation from the incarnation and his life of ministry, service, obedience and growth to perfection. "Son though he was, he learned obedience from what he suffered and once, made perfect, he became the source of eternal salvation for all who obey him" (Heb 5:8–9). The cross is important in order to achieve atonement but it is not the cross alone but the whole of Christ's life, including his suffering, that is essential and soteriologically significant. Similarly, for Christ's disciples perfection in Christ is not achieved apart from the circumstances of life.

On the one hand, one does not earn salvation simply by undergoing the minor stresses and great tragedies of life but, on the other hand, nor is one saved apart from them. The work of transformation and perfection in Christ takes place as part and parcel of the present life of the kingdom of God. When salvation is interpreted solely in terms of the death of Christ then it becomes largely a matter of dealing with the guilt of sin through justification by grace. In this context all the difficulties and sufferings of life that everyone faces are interpreted as a tragic dimension of life that is the result of the misuse of human free will, which not only led to the fall and a loss of the original state of perfection for humanity but also the subjection to futility and decay of the whole of creation (Rom 8:20). Those difficulties and challenges that remain are therefore perceived negatively as flaws in the present fabric of life, aspects of life that ought not be present and that will, indeed, one day be removed. Dealing with them is seen as important but as a part of our response to salvation rather than as part of salvation itself. The alternative is not to see these difficulties and challenges, great and small, merely as problems to be endured and ultimately overcome but, more positively, to see them as the essential tools that are to be used in becoming Christlike.

In God's world even that which is evil can be transformed into something good and, of course, the primary illustration of this is the cross of Christ, which was intended for evil by those who sought his death but which, through God's wisdom, achieved the greatest good for the world. Similarly, all that is intended for evil and all that produces suffering can be transformed and become a means of producing good. This needs to be qualified by the recognition that not everything that is evil will be transformed or revealed as good within the confines of this present age. But many things are transformed and it is possible to sees the various problems of this world more positively—as part of the challenging process of humanity being made perfect. Events that cause human suffering can be used, in the response of those affected, to reveal both the nature of God (and thus to show divine power and to encourage believers, 2 Cor 4:7–18) and the genuineness of the faith of believers (1 Pet 1:7; Jas 1:12). They can be the means of coming to repentance (2 Cor 7:5–13), a way of achieving maturity (Jas 5:3) and of obtaining blessing (Matt 5:10–12; 1 Pet 3:13–18).

This way of understanding the role of evil and disaster in the world is often referred to as a "soul-building" or "Irenaean" interpretation of the gospel, after Irenaeus of Lyons (c. 130–200).[6] According to this way of thinking humanity is made as part of God's good creation, and if "perfection" is to be used to describe humanity it is to be understood not in an absolute sense but more as an incomplete perfection in the sense that humanity is good and perfect but not yet what God intended—perhaps in the way that a rosebud can be perfect but is not yet the full flower that it is to become one day. Sin, then, is not so much a "fall" as the failure to develop; sin means not moving toward that form of life which God intended. Whereas in the aforementioned free will account there is a stress on the *guilt* of sin and the way in which justification through the death of Christ deals with it, in the soul-building account there is greater stress on the need to deal with the *effect* of sin in the life of the believer. This leads to a greater stress on the soteriological significance of the Christ's *life* as well as his *death*. Christ is the one who lived human life perfectly, and thus was able to come into the presence of the Father. Redemption therefore means that believers are incorporated into Christ and share the benefits of his life. Consequently, *when it comes to accounting for the myriad challenging struggles that people face in life* the soul-building approach sees the various problems more positively, not merely as the tragic element of life but also as part of the challenging process of humanity being made perfect. These difficulties and challenges, great and small, are the essential tools that are to be used in becoming Christlike. The suffering that comes from tragedy is a discipline that produces righteousness (Heb 12:3–10; John 15:2) and a way of imitating Christ (Phil 3:10).

In illustrating this let us consider one of the simplest forms of transformation—and one of the most extreme forms of suffering. At the simplest level the obvious observation is that the only way to learn patience is to be kept waiting. One would never learn anything about patience if it was never needed, if everything happened on time and if no one procrastinated or made mistakes that led to delays. Patience would not exist as it would not need to exist and no one would have any need of character development in that area of life. The irony is that perfect circumstances in regard to time would prevent the perfection of people. But if everything happened on time why should one be concerned about a lack of development of character in regard to time and patience in dealing with delays in it? Precisely because it would be a loss of character development, those who have learned to be patient have been blessed with growth that

---

6. Hick, *Evil and the God of Love*, 211–19.

has changed them; they are better *people* for having learned to relate well to other people. Indeed, those who know nothing of patience—or, by the same logic, nothing of love, joy, peace, patience, kindness, generosity or self-control, the biblical fruit of the Spirit (Gal 3:28)—are hardly people at all. They are biological, rather than mechanical, automatons—an imitation of humanity, robots without a soul. We develop character through hardship: we learn patience by being kept waiting, joy by dealing with sadness, peacefulness in the face of upset and violence, kindness from observing need and injustice, generosity from being in the presence of poverty, and inequality and self-control in aggravating circumstances.

But, one might ask, surely these qualities can be gained fairly easily, by learning to deal with minor problems; surely this way of thinking cannot account for the presence of the greatest tragedies—disaster, wars and persecution—of the world? I was once asked by someone who understood both free will and soul-building explanations of evil (the former saying that evil exists as a necessary result of the gift of free will, and the latter that evil exists as a means of developing the life of the soul) why God did not just get rid of the worst aspects of the world, the grossest forms of evil and injustice. Surely free will could still exist and spiritual growth take place without, for example, genocide? But the problem is that if God did make genocide impossible then something else would simply be the worst tragedy, and this new worst would be seen with exactly the same fear and trepidation as the former one. Whatever it is, there will always be a worst that represents the pinnacle of evil and challenges our ability to see good in what emerges.

In short, there is an agonistic element to the spiritual life that involves very serious play. Spiritual growth comes through challenge and struggle. It is by no means an easy game to play, and it may lead to frustration and even anger and despair. But even the most ordinary forms of play do not only involve joy and humor. Indeed, play is not a single mood. It may include laughter and singing, but even the simplest games may also include crying and shouting, apprehension and concern, frustration and sometimes pain. More serious games go much further to incorporate other moods and tenses without any loss of the agonistic game element. Play does not even run away from death, either in fantasy, role-playing and imagination or even, for some, in reality, because play has deep developmental purposes—perfecting the character and strengthening the soul. It is the way the self develops itself. It is important that there is no predictable outcome in terms of the game that is being played. It necessarily involves suspense and the unknown as well as danger and risk. This is essential and it results in a person who has the faith to be able to deal with suspense, failure, the unknown and uncertainty.

At the beginning of this chapter we noted that Bonhoeffer argued that it is not play of the ordinary kind that makes one happy, but one's happiness and security in Christ that enables one to play fully. But, as we have argued here, it is also play in the spiritual life that creates this faithfulness. The agonistic element of play in regard to the struggles of life is a preparation for that which is to come. It is the means to the development of character and an important part of the eschatological goal towards which all things are directed.

Playing with the Idea of Play

Playing Despite Circumstances

The connection of play with pain, suffering and ultimately with redemption is the area that is perhaps the most difficult and the most likely to be misunderstood. Choose a difficult area of life and try to see it in terms of some of the elements of play. And remember that not all play is trivial amusement; some forms of play are very serious and closely associated with challenge and risk—especially in children, where play is associated with moral and social development.

9

Kingdom: Playing with God

This is what the Lord says: "I will return to Zion and dwell in Jerusalem . . . the Faithful City . . . the Holy Mountain . . . The city streets will be filled with boys and girls playing there."

ZECHARIAH 8:3–5

Johann Christoph Friedrich von Schiller (1759–1805), apparently known to everyone as Fritz, was for a short while a rather reluctant physician who became better known as the poet whose "Ode to Joy" was made particularly famous by Beethoven's musical adaptation of it. He became a philosopher of aesthetics of some note, but is best known as one of Germany's great classical playwrights. Of relevance for our present purposes is the fact that he well understood that play lies at the heart of things and he commented (in the words of this unfortunately non-gender-inclusive English translation) that "man only plays when in the full meaning of the word he is a man, and he is only completely a man when he plays."[1]

This emerged from his understanding of aesthetics as the contemplation of the beautiful. Aesthetics is often seen, somewhat mistakenly, as the philosophy of art, and such philosophizing may be one of the consequences of the appreciation of the beautiful but it is not the primary focus. It is a particularly modern perspective in which the mind's—or the soul's—relationship with the beautiful is primarily logical, rational and philosophical. The classic understanding of this relationship is more *contemplatively* orientated; that is, we contemplate, for example, a rose as part of God's creation, a work of art as the product of human creativity or, finally, God

---

1. Schiller, *On the Aesthetic Education of Man*, 101–2.

as the ultimate beauty. Neither the beauty of the rose, the work of art, nor God can be grasped by mere logic and, therefore, before there can be a philosophical or analytical reflection put into theorems, words or formulae there needs to be a silent, contemplative apprehension of the beautiful in which the person is grasped by the beauty of the object of their contemplation. Schiller had a particular understanding of the aesthetic as the union of the sensuous and the rational, which, when seen corporately, leads towards a future utopian state, but one need not adopt this in its entirely in order to appreciate the related claim that the aesthetic dimension of human life is primarily expressed in the form of an impulse to play. This is because only play is completely free of utilitarian, moral, political purpose. It is that which is spontaneous and has intrinsic value; it is that which is enjoyed solely for its own sake. Thus, for Schiller, a relationship with the beautiful, with God, is—as the central argument of this book also puts it—best expressed in the concept of play.

Play may, of course, also have extrinsic value and purpose of such importance that it would be inappropriate to describe them as mere byproducts; nonetheless, they are secondary because when the contemplation and appreciation of God is undertaken for extrinsic purposes the relationship is subject to potential distortion and destruction. In that situation the beautiful—God—is being used for purposes other than the appreciation of God. But God is not to be used for other purposes; as the Westminster Shorter Catechism says, our chief purpose in life is "to glorify God and to enjoy him forever." Play is a primary image of the enjoyment of God and, as has been shown in the various chapters of this book, the major themes of Christian life and theology—Christ, faith, worship, spirituality, theology, grace, love, redemption and kingdom—are enriched by being expounded in the light of play. The relationship believers have with God in the present age ought to be characterized by play as well as by service and worship. But although it is an important element of our present relationship with God, it is even more central to the life of the future kingdom of God.

Living in the Kingdom

According to God's promise to the prophet Zechariah, Zion, the city of God, will one day be a city "filled with boys and girls playing" (Zech 8:5), and Martin Luther described the future kingdom of God as a time when people will "play with heaven and earth, the sun and all the creatures."

Indeed, he rejoices that all creation will play with God and everyone "shall have their fun, love and joy, and shall laugh with thee and thou with them."[2] It is generally the case that when Christians want to describe the character of life in the *future* kingdom of God they follow the example of Zechariah and Luther and employ the imagery of song and dance, play, laughter, joy and feasting. But of all these play is perhaps the most powerful expression of the life of the kingdom because this single image of children at play intrinsically embraces the innocence, joy, fun, laughter, celebration and communion of the other images. It powerfully—and surprisingly—expresses the true nature of life with God. This, of course, is very different to the language typically used to describe the character of an authentic Christian life in the *present*, which will more likely make reference to a life of faith, discipleship, commitment, service, sacrifice, ministry, mission and worship. One gets a very different impression of the character of kingdom life in the present compared to the future. But although there are some obvious differences between the two, Christians are frequently rightly reminded that the connection between them is also very real. The church is often described proleptically as a model, a sign, an anticipation or a present realization of the future kingdom, one that has been inaugurated in the ministry of Jesus and is realized in the church by the presence of the Holy Spirit. As Jesus said, the kingdom of God is "in your midst" (Luke 17:21) and, as part of the body of Christ, Christians are called to help make the future kingdom real in the present day.

Living eschatologically as a Christian means living out the future kingdom of God in the present. And it is precisely because Christians are called to represent the life of the future kingdom in this present world that it is so important to live with a playful attitude to God and the world. The life of the future should become real in the present. The responsibility of the church to be a model or microcosm of the future kingdom means nothing if it does not mean being the joyful people of God in the present. Christians are to bring this future joyful life into reality in the present and to "play it" this way *as though* the kingdom were present, because in and through the church and the working of the Spirit *it actually can become* real and present. While ministry, service and sacrifice are part and parcel of life in the present because the end of the present age has not yet come about, the truest expression of the life of the kingdom is not found in successful work or achievements in ministry as much as in the grace-filled expressions of joy,

2. Moltmann, *Theology of Play*, 36–37.

love, laughter and play that break into the present world and that ought to permeate Christian lives. These moments of joy are not merely moments of relief—they are anticipations of eternal life. They are the kingdom present. To really live out the kingdom means entering a completely new world of communion with God in joy and happiness.

All too often, however, it seems as though the present Christian life is about grace deferred. That is, the present life is seen as a time to be endured and worked through rather than enjoyed as we await the glorious, future kingdom of God. The present era is, indeed, a time that mixes joy and sorrow, pain and pleasure, tragedy and triumph as we await the final revelation of Christ in his glory, but this certainty of a future hope has implications for our understanding of the present time, for the kingdom is in the present as well as the future and the glory of God is revealed all around us at this very moment. As much as this world is a *preparation* for the next it is also a present *demonstration* of that life of play, dance, music, joy and rejoicing. The biblical images of life in the eternal kingdom of God are not ones that stress or glorify human achievement; instead they focus on childlike play and joy, and we are able to experience a foretaste of the future eschatological life as we share in this playful joy in the present.

Nonetheless, although one can always find elements of this joyfulness in the life of the church, one might wonder whether it is sufficiently to the fore in the lives of believers or in the thinking and teaching of pastors and theologians. In describing the Christian life the general stress certainly seems to fall on other themes, especially those that stress the challenge, the cost and the commitment involved in being a disciple. It often appears that joy and laughter and a playful attitude are appropriate for children but that it is more appropriate for the one who wants to become a mature Christian to focus on the significance of the sacrifice of Christ and the cost of discipleship. Christian maturity, it seems, brings with it a more sober and serious attitude to ministry, mission and service. As a result of this widespread consensus it is therefore perhaps a theologically risky undertaking to suggest that this needs to be reconsidered. There is, of course, absolutely no doubt that these challenging themes of discipleship are critically important dimensions of the Christian life; nonetheless, it is well worth reassessing the situation and asking whether there are not certain factors that resist or downplay the true significance of the playful and joyful elements of the kingdom of God.

A tendency to downplay the playfulness of the kingdom can be seen in various ways. Firstly, it happens when the present Christian life is characterized solely in terms of service, sacrifice, obedience and faithful ministry without sufficient reference to joy, celebration, pleasure or play. Service, sacrifice and ministry are critically important ways in which Christians express their faith in God and live out the life of the kingdom but they ought not be allowed to exclude joy and laughter. The nature of the Christian life should not be influenced by cultural factors that stress the virtue of work over play. Life is misunderstood if it is only seen in terms of *working for* God; it is important to learn to *play and dance with* God as well. Obedience and duty, sacrifice, service and self-giving need to be complemented with play and pleasure, joy and appreciation. Indeed, the term "the kingdom," by which, in shorthand fashion, Christians identify the reign of God, the lordship of Christ and the presence of the Spirit both present and future, could easily be replaced by reference to "the party." If that were to become part of Christian terminology it would point much more clearly towards the play, joy and laughter that are essential, central parts of the future life that Christians are called to live in the present.

Secondly, there can also be a downplaying of the playfulness of the kingdom when the future Christian life is characterized either in terms of judgment or as an eternal rest that simply involves the removal of sin and suffering and relief from earthly labor. The characterization of eternal life as being an eternal rest is an important part of Christian hope, a promise that believers frequently hold to very dearly. The well-known passage in the Revelation of John says that at the time of the new heaven and new earth "He will wipe every tear from their eyes. There will be no more death or mourning or crying or pain, for the old order of things has passed away" (21:4). But the absence of pain and suffering needs to be complemented with an understanding of a presence of God that is more than an absence, or a passive, static rest or a quiet, earnest, serious relationship. In fact, the notion of "communion with God" should be positively expressed in terms of glorious, joyful engagement. The lordship of Christ, the revelation of the sovereignty of God and the exercise of justice are rightly seen as important to an understanding of the return of Christ but these occur precisely in order to bring about an ongoing state of eternal playfulness, joy and communion with God. For some believers the significance of this succinct statement of purpose—that we are to simply enjoy God forever—is lost because it is too difficult to imagine the King of kings or the Judge of all as playing around and having a laugh. The former imagery seems more appropriate and respectful than the latter.

These are, of course, usually unconscious errors that are simply the result of stressing one aspect of the Christian life more than another, often influenced by other factors, such as those cultural mores that stress work more than play and authority more than relationships. Service, sacrifice and ministry are critically important ways in which Christians express their faith in God and live out the life of the kingdom but in biblical imagery the final state of life for the believer is not characterized in terms of work, ministry, service or sacrifice but in terms of joy, gladness, laughter and play.

The imagery at this point is more aesthetic than ethical in focus, and more child-focused than adult. Play, dance, joy and laughter are essential, central parts of the future life that Christians are called to live in the present. It is very important, therefore, to help Christians understand and express their new life in Christ in terms of intimate, joyful, playful relationship with him as well as in terms of obedient service and sacrifice. The latter may initially appear more noble and more worthy of encouragement, but the former express even more radically the amazing grace of God. And it is not only the world that needs to see these qualities expressed, but the believer does as well because without the joy, play and laughter of intimate relationship obedient service and sacrifice easily becomes a formal obligation or a legal responsibility rather than a joyful sharing. And consequently God becomes more a distant Master to be obeyed than a close Friend to be loved.

An emphasis on this kind of spiritual life will, of course, appear either absurd or idealistic to those who are fixed within a framework of work and ministry. While nothing said here should be taken as minimizing the importance of ministry, justice, sacrifice or suffering for Christ, nonetheless, these are not the end towards which the kingdom is moving. Hitherto life has been subject to both sin itself and to the work of overcoming the effects of sin, injustice, pain and suffering, but through Christ and the presence of the Holy Spirit life is eventually liberated, sin is overcome and life is released into joyful play. This means that the present life of the church will not only necessarily involve labor, ministry and sacrifice but also ought to be understood as involving clear anticipations of the future life of joy, for in Christ life is liberated into joyfulness and playfulness. This playfulness is not to be found so much in specific playful activities that are engaged in from time to time as much as in an *attitude* of mind that produces a playful approach to the whole of life. Those who have this ability to find the playful dimension in all aspects of life find it enriched. The ability to find the creative, playful dimension of work, friendships, family relationships, community service and so forth is a real blessing and in this way God's playful kingdom can break into the world at any time.

One of the most common metaphors for the Christian life is that of life as a journey and, more specifically, as a pilgrimage. This is imagery that has a definite purpose, an end, a destination. It resonates well with certain themes involving an eschatological purpose, heaven, a new creation, a final consummation. But taken purely by itself it can represent life as simply a task to be done, a road to be travelled with the sole purpose of arriving at the end. This can lead to a neglect of the present life in favor of an anticipation of that which is to come. Another image for the Christian life is that of listening and playing music. In this case getting to the end of the music is not the point. A good ending is very satisfying and enriching but its meaning is not found in its ending. And there is no point in wanting to get to the end quickly; indeed, racing to the end can destroy the experience of it. It is in the playing and the enjoyment of the music that its meaning is found. The challenge here is to live life in such a way that every moment is appreciated and enjoyed.

The Dance of Life

Song and dance are both joyful expressions of the life of the future kingdom of God that ought to present in the life of the church. As the psalmist said, "Sing to the Lord a new song . . . Let Israel rejoice in their Maker; let the people of Zion be glad in their King. Let them praise his name with dancing" (Ps 149: 1–3). Unfortunately, while congregational singing has been much appreciated, dance has not been so popular. Indeed, dance, like other forms of playfulness, has had image problems within the church and has typically been seen as rather worldly. It has been suggested that the real answer to the question "Why are Baptists (or if you prefer, Methodists or Presbyterians) against extramarital sex?" is "Because it might lead to dancing!" There have been times, it must be admitted, when dancing has been viewed more positively. Although there is no biblical imagery of God dancing, nor does Christ dance (except in the apocryphal second-century *Acts of John*, which recounts the way in which Jesus commanded the apostles to form a circle around him and dance as he sang a hymn), parts of the church in the Christian Roman Empire nonetheless did incorporate ritual dance in worship at churches and at shrines. Paul Dilley has shown that in the Roman era many texts such as the Coptic *Dance of the Savior* were produced and promoted by bishops and that liturgical dancing was a part of many festivals.[3] One problem, however, with dance in worship, which led to some reserve concerning it, was that it could be associated with pagan practices. The easy connection that can be made between dancing and sensuality inevitably leads to suspicion, but the dangers involved in these inappropriate connotations cannot undermine the fundamental appropriateness of understanding that a God of joy and love, of exuberance and happiness, would appreciate and approve of and, metaphorically, even participate in dancing. And even that dangerous association with sensuality can rightly express the intimacy, closeness and participation in the life of God that believers experience in their relationship with God. Dance, like play and music and singing, is a theologically appropriate expression of the joyful, pleasurable, dynamic relationships that God has, both with people and in intra-Trinitarian life. Dance and play are expressions both of the inner relationship between Father, Son and Spirit and of the possibility of human participation in that relationship.

The metaphor of dance helps here because the doctrine of the Trinity is completely misunderstood if it is seen merely as a formal definition of divine nature rather than as *the actual experience of a living Christian faith*. John Wesley understood this and argued that in formal discussions of the Trinity the use of particular terms such as "Trinity" or "persons" is not of great significance but, he said, it is essential that the believer has *the experience* of the Trinitarian life of God.[4] He made it clear that the concept of the Trinity is not only an intellectual belief but the foundation of a vital spiritual life. As it has been said, the Trinity is not a toy for theologians but a joy for believers. Indeed, the doctrine of the Trinity is primarily known by experiencing God as Father, Son and Spirit rather than by comprehending it by rational thought. There is, in fact, a paradox here, that we understand the Trinity most when we realize that we only understand it dimly. If we think that the doctrine of Trinity is entirely something of the mind and try to work it out along purely rational lines then we are altogether mistaken. Fortunately, one of the most important aspects of the biblical imagery of the future life with God is that it tells us that *the life of God as Trinity is something in which we participate*. It may

3. Dilley, "Jesus as Lord of the Dance."
4. Wesley, *Works*, Sermon 55.

be impossible to fully grasp with the mind but it is a life that can be lived or even, as some have said, a dance to be enjoyed.

In that regard the term "perichoresis" (meaning "interpenetration," "circumincession" or "mutual indwelling") has been used theologically at least since the time of John of Damascus (c. 675–749) to refer to the way in which the three divine persons live in joyful, dynamic communion without merging or loss of distinction. It is said to be derived from the Greek term *perichoreuō*, meaning "to dance around." However, the evidence indicates that the term is derived from the different though very similar-looking word *perichōreō*, which has the sense of "interpenetration" but does not refer to dancing.[5] Although one cannot, therefore, turn to the etymology of perichoresis for support for the image of a dancing God, this does not mean that the concept itself is inappropriate, as evidenced by those who appreciate its use in that way. Nor does one have to rely on the word of the atheist Friedrich Nietzsche, who famously declared that he would only believe in a God who danced,[6] even though he may have had a good point. Scriptural affirmation of dancing comes from the Psalms, which exhort dancing in praise of God, and at various times the prophetess Miriam and King David are described as doing exactly that. And the word of the Lord through Jeremiah was that all the people of Israel would dance when God came to rescue them from exile.[7]

This participatory dimension of the Trinitarian life of God whereby the triune relationships are an expression of a divine life that is open to others is revealed when the Trinity is explored *eschatologically* as well as *essentially* and *economically*, as has been the case at least since Karl Rahner (1904–1984) debated the relationship between the "economic Trinity" and the "essential (or immanent) Trinity."[8] There is, of course, only one Trinity and the term "economic" is a simply a reference to the way it is possible to understand the Trinity in terms of God's economy or work of salvation. That is, the Trinity derives from God's work as creator, Christ's work as redeemer and the Spirit's work in applying salvation to the whole world. God is involved in all three and so there is a tri-unity. In short, God's triune nature is revealed in God's salvific work within the created order. On the

---

5. Peterson, *Christ Plays in Ten Thousand Places*, 44–45; and LaCugna, *God for Us*, 271.

6. Nietzsche, *Thus Spoke Zarathustra*, 29.

7. Ps 30:11; 149:3; 150:1–6; Exod 15:20; 2 Sam 6:14; Jer 31:13.

8. Rahner, *Trinity*, 101.

other hand, the "essential Trinity" is a reference to the way the Trinity can be understood in terms of divine *relationships*, rather than divine *work*. That is, the Trinity is known as God the Father of Jesus, Jesus the Son of the Father and the Spirit who, as the creeds say, "proceeds" from the Father and (or "through") the Son. The conclusion, known as Rahner's Rule, is "that the economic Trinity is the immanent Trinity, and the immanent Trinity is the economic Trinity," indicating that what God reveals in the salvific work of the Trinity genuinely reflects the actual inner divine nature. But there is a sense in which this dramatic and relational understanding of the *economic* and *essential* Trinity needs to incorporate a third, *eschatological* dimension, which shows the way in which, in the final kingdom, the Trinitarian life of God incorporates an interpersonal depth and joyous intimacy of relationship with the people of God, which is best represented through the imagery of play and dance. And there is a need not only to reflect on what this playing and dancing with God means *for people*, but also to reflect on what it means *for God's Trinitarian nature*. How do intimate, warm, close, interactive, joyful relationships affect God?

The doctrine of the Trinity and, specifically, its participatory nature distinguishes Christian faith from all other forms of religious belief, including other monotheistic faiths. Indeed, a participatory understanding of the Trinity is radically different from the all-too-frequent nominally Trinitarian conviction that, in practice, perceives God in a purely monotheistic and not genuinely trinitarian fashion. This occurs when the Christian God is understood to be an infinite, eternal being who is essentially distinct from humanity and known only externally, as one knows another person from a distance, as a subject knows a king or as a servant knows a master. Unfortunately, some Christian faith only goes this far in its understanding of the relationship between the believer and God. But when experientially understood the doctrine of the Trinity goes beyond understanding God as one who is known at a distance, as a King, Master or Lord (not that these are inappropriate!), and presents the possibility of a far more intimate relationship that not only involves the possibility of *coming closer* to God (using, for example, the metaphors of Friend, Father and Lover), but also of *uniting with* God in union, communion and participation. Or, more imaginatively, we may think of God as a dance partner or playful companion rather than (or perhaps as well as) as King or Master.

The point of this imagery is that the life of holiness to which God calls us is a joining in, a participation, an experience of playing together, singing and dancing with God. And, as has been suggested, this playing and dancing together is not only important for people but it is also important for God. The mutuality of the imagery of play and dance implies that God also takes pleasure in this dynamic relationship. Those who prefer formal theological language will refer to this as *theosis*—union with God—but those who prefer more imaginative language will understand this in terms of divine playfulness and dance in which all participate. One might say that this is "the hokey-pokey theory of Trinitarian theology." That is, it is a dance where, in the end, "you put your whole self in." Understood in this way God as Trinity not only meets with believers but also takes in, surrounds and eternally sustains them. Life is lived *within* the dynamic, three-personed life of God who, importantly, is not unaffected by these relationships. This conviction needs to be expressed carefully because God's life is not dependent upon or created by the life of others. But nor is God unmoved, uncaring or unaffected by them. This mysterious, wonderful participation between God and humanity is a consequence of the coming together of human and divine in the person of Jesus Christ and through the presence of the Holy Spirit in the world today.

This union is expressed by the biblical writers in a number of different ways and with varying emphases. The gospel of John, for example, focuses on union with not only Jesus the incarnate Son ("you will abide in my love") but also with the Father ("as you, Father, are in me and I am in you, may they also be in us") and the Spirit ("When the Advocate comes whom I will send to you from the Father, the Spirit of truth who comes from the Father, he will testify on my behalf" (15:15; 17:21; 15:26). The epistle to the Ephesians speaks of the notion of *anakephalaiōsasthai*, the "gathering together" by which the whole cosmos comes "under" the head of Christ. The Father reveals "the mystery of his will" to be "put into effect when the times reach their fulfillment," namely, "to bring unity to all things in heaven and on earth under Christ" (1:9–10). It refers to nothing short of cosmic reunification in Christ. All things point to Christ—he is the focal point of the whole of creation—and Paul urges people to bring their lives into conformity with God's divine plan so that Christ is central in everything that they do. The final illustration of this union with God is found in 2 Peter 1:4, which speaks of the "great and precious promises" of God, "so that through them you may participate in the divine nature and escape the corruption in the world caused by evil desires." This "participation in the divine nature" does not turn people into God nor make

God dependent upon people but it locates redeemed life and relationships within the Trinitarian life of God. God does not exist within the world—as though the world were the greater concept—rather, *the world and human life actually exist within God*, embraced by divine love and experienced as part of the inner Trinitarian life of God.

This experiential, participatory understanding of consummation life is a reminder that the future is not so much a *place* as an *existence in God*. The life of the Trinity is an interpersonal fellowship in which believers participate by grace and that has significance for God. If we try to understand the significance of the eschaton apart from its significance for God then we really cannot grasp it. The meaning of the eschaton is tied up with the future eschatological life of God. At the end, the love of God is victorious; it is the end of tears and suffering (Rev 21:4) and God enters into fellowship with the whole creation. It is precisely in God that all things come together and so there is, then, as a result "one God and Father of all, who is over all and through all and in all" (Eph 1:10; 4:6). One of the reasons that dance, like play, is such a good metaphor is that it expresses the dynamism, the joy and the intimate interaction of the relationship. Dance and play involve dancing and playing *together*, expressing communion, sharing, mutual pleasure and the fulfillment of love and desire. Indeed, all dance and play arises from a human longing for the community and joy that, in the end, are truly found only in God and so the final, eschatological kingdom of God is well expressed as a time of great joy and intimacy, of singing, dancing and play.

The notion of people "playing with God" is one that is less frequently heard than that of people "playing God." The latter is typically a disapproving reference to those who make ethical decisions that, it is thought, should be left to God alone to make. So those who are involved with making decisions about, for example, genetic engineering or abortion are criticized for taking on what might to be divine responsibilities. This typically overlooks both the *biblical* argument that humanity, as bearers of the image of God, has a God-given responsibility to "represent" God (to exercise dominion or stewardship) in the world and the *logical* point that doing nothing is just as much an active decision that will lead to some outcome as intervening. The real ethical question is not whether to act but what kind of action to take. This ethical focus on "playing God" is very different from "playing with God," which is a representation of the theological notion of life as participation with God. Being called to play with God is one part of the amazing paradoxes of the faith. The Creator becomes a part of the creation. The one who is Lord and Master of the universe becomes a friend of people. The living God has a Son who dies. The Transcendent One engages in close, intimate relationships. God the righteous, holy one wants relationships characterized by play, joy and laughter. Within this serious life, as part of ministry and service, there is also a game going on in which it is possible to engage with God and enrich one's life. Discerning this game in the present helps us look forward with joy and hope to the ultimate play of the future kingdom.

There is no trivialization in saying that life, death and resurrection are all part of the playful purpose of life. Even death is a part of this great and wonderful game. Some games involve very little uncertainty and minimal risk. They are safe and not risky, enjoyable and not threatening. But other games, such as mountaineering and wingsuit flying, are adventures that involve significant risk and even personal danger. These games have the greatest challenges and while every game has a degree of uncertainty about the outcome these games can have high levels of uncertainty about even the kind of outcome that could eventuate. These games are challenges and are not necessarily safe at all. Injury and even death are possible outcomes and, because of this, they are often avoided and not seen as mere play but as something much more serious. But simply *living* always involves dying. Death is always a part of the greatest game of all. It cannot be avoided and learning to live with death is an essential part of life. Playing this game well and successfully means playing it with God. This is a game played as part of a team, and it means trusting one's partner. Indeed, as in all team games, the whole focus needs to be not on the game as such but on the people involved and on the relationships that are developed. While the real, central point of playing is always for the sake of playing rather than for utilitarian purposes, the point of the play is not the game itself but the experience of playing and learning something about oneself and the others with whom one is playing. Especially when the other is God.

In some games every possible move is known in advance and the only issue is the sequence of the moves. When someone else is involved this can be very complicated but the right sequence will ultimately lead to success. But in other games, such as games of make-believe, the moves and the possibilities are much greater. Some games do not specify the moves or the actions that *are* permitted but only specify what may *not* happen (such as, do not say, "That light saber is not real; it's only a stick!"), leaving the direction of the game much more open to the imagination and the creative play of the participants. These games can contain unexpected twists as players devise new and creative moves or actions. God has made some unexpected and exciting moves in the game of life and death, extending from the trivial (such as the game played in getting me to write this book[9]) to the most dramatic (such as raising Christ from the dead!), and in so doing has revealed more and more of his character to us. Each person plays with God in this game and, as in all games, can share in the pleasure of play and the joy of sharing with another. This is a game that begins in the present life and extends through death into the future life with God, and as such it is an eternal game. That does not mean it is simply unending, for eternity is beyond the categories of time and space, but is better understood as referring to a new and different quality of playing to which we can look forward. But learning to discern play in the present world is part of one's growth in holiness—understanding more deeply the nature of God. As G. K. Chesterton put it,

> It is not only possible to say a great deal in praise of play; it is really possible to say the highest things in praise of it. It might reasonably be maintained that the true object of all human life is play. Earth is a task garden; heaven is a playground. To be at last in such secure innocence that one can juggle with the universe and the stars, to be so good that one can treat everything as a joke—that may be, perhaps, the real end and final holiday of human souls. When we are really holy we may regard the Universe as a lark.[10]

A playful attitude, I suggest, lies at the very heart of all spirituality and is critical for the whole of life. It will enrich our lives if we come to see that play is the essential and ultimate form of relationship with God.

9. See chapter 1.

10. Chesterton, *All Things Considered*, 40.

Playing with the Idea of Play

Playing with Imagination and the Future

It is because Christians are called to represent the life of the future kingdom in this present world that it is so important to live with a playful attitude toward God and the world. In this playful exercise you should begin by imagining (perhaps over a period of days) whatever you can about the life of the future kingdom of God. It might be difficult to imagine what it will "look" like, so try and focus on what it will "feel" like in terms of joy, pleasure, communion and so forth. Then shift the focus of your imagination to the present day and ask, "What would be involved if this or that aspect of the future kingdom (whatever you had been reflecting about) was to be made real in this present time and place?" What would need to take place for that to happen? What can be done to make it even partially real?

Bibliography

Aquinas, Thomas. *The Summa Theologica*. Translated by English Dominicans. Chicago: Encyclopaedia Britannica, 1955.

Augustine of Hippo. *Confessions*. Translated by R. S. Pine-Coffin. London: Penguin, 1961.

Barth, Karl. *Church Dogmatics*. Vol. II–I. Translated by T. H. L. Parker, W. B. Johnston, H. Knight, and J. L. M. Haire. Edinburgh: T. & T. Clark, 1956.

Baxter, Richard. *A Christian Directory: A Sum of Practical Theology and Cases of Conscience, 1838*. Orlando, FL: Ligonier Ministries, 1996.

Bennett, Willis. "Play and Its Meaning for Preaching." *Review and Expositor* 47/2 (April 1950) 165–72.

Benzie, Peter. "As a Little Child: Children in the Theology of John Wesley." MTh diss., Laidlaw-Carey Graduate School, 2010.

Bonhoeffer, Dietrich. *Letters and Papers from Prison*. Translated by Reginald Fuller et al. Edited by Eberhard Bethge. Enlarged ed. New York: Touchstone, 1997.

Brown, Stuart, with Christopher Vaughan. *Play: How It Shapes the Brain, Opens the Imagination, and Invigorates the Soul*. Kindle ed. Carlton North, Victoria: Scribe, 2010.

Caillois, Roger. *Man and the Sacred*. Translated by Meyer Barash. Urbana: University of Illinois Press, 2001.

———. *Man, Play and Games*. Translated by Meyer Barash. Urbana: University of Illinois Press, 2001. Originally published 1961.

Calvin, John. *Institutes of the Christian Religion*. Translated by Ford Lewis Battles. Edited by John T. McNeill. 2 vols. London: Westminster, 1961.

Chagall, Marc, illustrator. *The Bible: Genesis, Exodus, The Song of Solomon*. San Francisco: Chronicle, 2005.

Chesterton, G. K. *All Things Considered*. Charleston, SC: BiblioBazaar, 2007.

Chrysostom, John. *Homilies on the Gospel of St. Matthew*. In vol. 10 of *Nicene and Post-Nicene Fathers*, series 1, edited by Philip Schaff. Grand Rapids: Eerdmans, 1988.

Dahl, Gordon. *Work, Play and Worship in a Leisure-Oriented Society*. Minneapolis: Augsburg, 1972.

Derrida, Jacques. "Structure, Sign, and Play in the Discourse of the Human Sciences." In *Writing and Difference*, translated by Alan Bass, 278–93. Chicago: University of Chicago Press, 1978.

Dilley, Paul. "Jesus as Lord of the Dance." *Bible History Daily*, August 8, 2014. https://www.biblicalarchaeology.org/daily/biblical-topics/post-biblical-period/jesus-as-lord-of-the-dance/.

Edgar, Brian. *God Is Friendship: A Theology of Spirituality, Community, and Society.* Wilmore, KY: Seedbed, 2013.

———. "Play." In *Dictionary of Scripture and Ethics*, edited by Joel B. Green et al., 595–96. Grand Rapids: Baker Academic, 2011.

Erasmus, Desiderious. *The Praise of Folly.* Translated by John Wilson. Edited P. S. Allen. Oxford: Clarendon, 1913.

Evans, James H., Jr. *Playing.* Minneapolis: Fortress, 2010.

Frost, Joe L. *A History of Children's Play and Play Environments: Toward a Contemporary Child Saving Movement.* New York: Routledge, 2010.

Frankl, Viktor Emil. *Man's Search for Meaning.* Translated by Ilse Lasch and Helen Pisano. Boston: Beacon, 2006.

Guardini, Romano. *The Spirit of the Liturgy.* Translated by Ada Lane. Reprint ed. New York: Crossroad, 1988.

Hippolytus of Rome. *The Refutation of All Heresies.* In vol. 5 of *Ante-Nicene Fathers*, edited by Alexander Roberts and James Donaldson. New York: Christian Literature, 1884.

Hopkins, Gerard Manley. *Poems of Gerard Manley Hopkins.* Edited by Robert Bridges. London: Humphrey Milford, 1918.

Huizinga, Johan. *Homo Ludens: A Study of the Play-Element in Culture.* Boston: Beacon, 1955.

International Theological Commission. *The Hope of Salvation for Infants Who Die without Being Baptised.* Vatican, 2007. http://www.vatican.va/roman_curia/congregations/cfaith/cti_documents/rc_con_cfaith_doc_20070419_un-baptised-infants_en.html.

Johnson, Steven. *Wonderland: How Play Made the Modern World.* New York: Riverhead, 2016.

Johnston, Robert K. *The Christian at Play.* Grand Rapids: Eerdmans, 1983.

Kane, Pat. *The Play Ethic: A Manifesto for a Different Way of Living.* London: Macmillan, 2004.

Thérèse of Lisieux. *Autobiography of a Saint.* Translated by Ronald Arbuthnott Knox. London: Collins, 1905.

LaCugna, Catherine M. *God for Us: The Trinity and Christian Life.* San Francisco HarperOne, 1993.

Ladinsky, Daniel, translator. *I Heard God Laughing: Poems of Hope and Joy: Renderings of Hafiz.* New York: Penguin, 2006.

Locke, John. *Some Thoughts Concerning Education and Of the Conduct of Understanding.* edited by Ruth Grant and Nathan Tarcov. Indianapolis: Hackett, 1996.

Louth, Andrew. *Maximus the Confessor.* Early Church Fathers. New York: Routledge, 1996.

Maximus the Confessor. *Ambigua.* Patrologiae cursus completus: Series graeca 91, edited by J. P. Migne. Paris: Imprimerie Catholique, 1865.

Miller, David LeRoy. *Gods and Games: Toward a Theology of Play.* New York: Harper, 1973.

Moltmann, Jürgen, et al. *Theology of Play*. Translated by Reinhard Ulrich. New York: Harper, 1972.

Neale, Robert E. "The Crucifixion as Play." In *Theology of Play*, by Jürgen Moltmann et al., translated by Reinhard Ulrich, 76–86. New York: Harper & Row, 1972.

———. *In Praise of Play: Toward a Psychology of Religion*. New York: Harper, 1969.

Nietzsche, Friedrich. *Thus Spoke Zarathustra: A Book for All and None*. Translated by Adrian Del Caro. Edited by Adrian Del Caro and Robert Pippen. Cambridge University Press, 2006.

Pannenberg, Wolfhart. *Systematic Theology*. Vol. 3. Grand Rapids: Eerdmans, 1998.

Peterson, Eugene H. *Christ Plays in Ten Thousand Places: A Conversation in Spiritual Theology*. Grand Rapids: Eerdmans, 2005.

Plato. *Cratylus*. In *Plato in Twelve Volumes*, translated by R. G. Bury, vol. 4. Cambridge, MA: Harvard University Press, 1967–1968.

———. *Laws*. In *Plato in Twelve Volumes*, translated by R. G. Bury, vols. 10–11. Cambridge, MA: Harvard University Press, 1967, 1968.

Power, Pat. "Playing with Ideas: The Effective Dynamics of Creative Play." *American Journal of Play* 3/3 (Winter 2011) 288–323.

Rahner, Hugo. *Man at Play, or, Did You Ever Practise Eutrapelia?* London: Burns & Oates, 1965.

Rahner, Karl. *The Trinity*. Translated by Joseph Donceel. New York: Herder, 1970.

Rousseau, Jean-Jacques. *The Émile of Jean-Jacques Rousseau*. Translated by William Boyd. York: Columbia University Press, 1965.

Schiller, Friedrich. *On the Aesthetic Education of Man*. Translated and edited by Elizabeth Mary Wilkinson and Leonard Ashley Willoughby. Oxford: Clarendon, 1967.

Screech, Michael A. *Laughter at the Foot of the Cross*. Boulder, CO: Westview, 1999.

Seuss, Dr. *The Cat in the Hat Comes Back!* New York: Random House, 1958.

Smedes, Lewis B. "Theology and the Playful Life." In *God and the Good: Essays in Honor of Henry Stob*, edited by Clifton Orlebeke and Lewis B. Smedes, 46–62. Grand Rapids: Eerdmans, 1975.

Sutton-Smith, Brian. *The Ambiguity of Play*. Cambridge, MA: Harvard University Press, 1997.

———. "Play Theory: A Personal Journey and New Thoughts." *American Journal of Play* 1/1 (Summer 2008) 80–123.

Torrance, James. *Worship, Community, and the Triune God of Grace*. Downers Grove, IL: InterVarsity, 1996.

Vaihinger, Hans. *The Philosophy of "As-If": A System of the Theoretical, Practical and Religious Fictions of Mankind*. Translated by C. K. Ogden. New York: Barnes and Noble, 1924.

Watson, J. R. *An Annotated Anthology of Hymns*. Oxford: Oxford University Press, 2002.

Watts, Isaac. *The Poems of Watts*. The Works of the English Poets 46. London: Hett, MDCCLXXIX.

Wesley, John. *The Journal of John Wesley*. Edited by Percy Livingstone Parker. Moody. Chicago: 1951.

———. "Sermon 50" and "Sermon 55." In *The Works of the Rev. John Wesley, A.M., Sometime Fellow of Lincoln College, Oxford*. London: Wesleyan-Methodist Book-Room, 1881.

———. "A Short Account of the School in Kingswood, Near Bristol." In *The Works of John Wesley,* vol. 13, *Letters,* edited by Thomas Jackson. 3rd ed., 1872. Reprint, Grand Rapids: Baker, 2007.

Witherington, Ben, III. *The Rest of Life: Rest, Play, Easting, Studying, Sex from a Kingdom Perspective.* Grand Rapids: Eerdmans, 2012.

Subject Index

Name Index

Abraham, 55, 90–91
Ambrose, of Milan, 4, 60
Angie, 96–97
Anselm, 105
Aquinas, Thomas. See Thomas Aquinas.
Aristotle, 3, 10, 61
Augustine, 10, 17, 19, 38, 60, 74, 103

Barth, Karl, 59
Baxter, Richard, 4, 78
Beethoven, Ludwig van, 113,
Bennett, Willis, 83
Bonhoeffer, Dietrich, 101–4, 112
Brown, Stuart, 26n1, 43, 65

Caillois, Roger, 65, 69–71
Calvin, John, 75, 77–78
Chagall, Marc, 88
Chesterton, G. K., 1, 6, 9–10, 62, 126
Chrysostom, John, 4, 74
Clement X, Pope, 39

Dahl, Gordon, 84
David, King, 30, 34, 90, 121
Dilley, Paul, 120
Duns Scotus, 19

Eckhardt, Meister, 3
Edgar, Brian, 7n13, 48n5
Erasmus, Desiderius, 59
Erikson, Erik, 12
Evans, James H., 37, 38n8
Ezra, 87

Frankl, Viktor, 24
Freud, Sigmund, 12
Frost, Joe L., 82

Gadamer, Hans–Georg, 3
Green, Joel, 7
Gregory the Great, 19
Gregory, of Nazianzus, 18
Gregory, of Nyssa, 18, 38
Guardini, Romano, 4, 27,

Hafiz (Shams–ud din Muhammad), 56
Heidegger, Martin, 3
Heraclitus, of Ephesus, 14–15
Herbert, George, 76
Hippolytus, of Rome, 14n1, 15, 30,
Hopkins, Gerard Manley, 26, 30–31
Huizinga, Johan, 1, 26n1, 7, 51–52, 53n9,
    61, 63–66, 69, 70, 72, 107

Irenaeus, of Lyons, 110
Isaac, 90–92

Jacob, 55–56, 90–91, 94
Jerome, Saint, 19
Jesus, Christ, x, 1, 3–5, 9, 14–23, 25–26,
    29–31, 36–40, 42, 45, 48–49, 50,
    56, 60, 73, 86–99, 101, 103–6,
    108–10, 112, 114–19, 120n3,
    121n5, 123, 126
John, of Damascus, 121
John, the Baptist, 15–17, 48, 93
John, the disciple, 45, 90, 92, 94–95,
    98–99, 117, 119, 123

Scripture Index

CPSIA information can be obtained
at www.ICGtesting.com
Printed in the USA
LVHW092202170121
676760LV00025B/300